"I have been a terrible breather—a chronic hyperventilator when I get tired and stressed—for my entire life. And then I met Ashley: She taught me how to focus on the exhale, to fully empty my lungs—and in the process, she gave me back control over this issue that has plagued my adult life."

—ELISE LOEHNEN, chief content officer, goop

"Living in 'survival mode' in our 24/7 world has health consequences on our moods, weight, hormones, immune system—even our outlook on life. The breath is the most important tool we have for finding and sustaining inner calm. *How to Breathe* is a beautiful touchstone filled with simple practices that can help you to shift quickly from feeling overwhelmed, out of balance, and frazzled into a sense of well-being—something we all want more of in this day and time."

—AVIVA ROMM, MD, author, *The Adrenal Thyroid Revolution*

"The modern world is moving ever-so-fast, and we are experiencing the effects within ourselves, and without. Not leaving us unaided or without answers, Ashley Neese graciously responds to our essential need to sustain our well-being in *How To Breathe*. This is a necessary text for our modern, steadily changing times."

—LALAH DELIA, founder, *Vibrate Higher Daily*

HOW TO

breathe

*To my younger self, who fought
so hard and for so long to inhabit
her body.*

*To anyone who has struggled to
be with themselves.*

*To all those who cultivate the
space to exhale.*

*To the ever-expanding desire for
presence.*

*To the life force that pulses
through each and every breath.*

To resilience.

HOW TO
breathe

25 simple practices
for calm, joy, and resilience

Ashley Neese

photography by anaïs & dax

TEN SPEED PRESS
California | New York

CONTENTS

Let's Begin:

25

Breathwork Practices

41

INTRODUCTION

to Breathwork

What do yoga, meditation, and forest bathing have in common? The breath.

The breath is the foundation of every mindfulness practice. It is the tool that's always with us, accessible at any time for calm, balance, and presence of mind. The amazing thing is that anybody—regardless of age, ability, location, or beliefs—can utilize breathwork to better navigate life. It just requires practice and attention. In essence, breathwork is breathing practiced with mindfulness. It's that simple.

Because of its accessibility and effectiveness, breathwork is quickly on the rise in the wellness field. Over the last decade, it has become an increasingly popular method of natural healing for anxiety, depression, PTSD, trauma, and chronic physical pain. It is also a practical tool for amplifying creativity, tapping into inner wisdom, and expanding consciousness. With science-backed breath labs set up at Stanford University and apps like Spire that detect your respiration rate throughout the day, it's clear that breathwork is reaching far beyond yoga and meditation, carving out its own space in the world.

Breathing is easy to take for granted because it's automatic. It's also easy to write off breathwork and think, "That's too simple—it won't work for me." Simple as it is, adopting a breath practice helps you cultivate greater health in all aspects of your life, from relationships to work to stress to grief.

I came to the breath the way many of us do, through meditation and yoga. I started meditating out of necessity in a drug rehab when I was twenty-one. At the time I was involved in a twelve-step program and had a sponsor who encouraged me to learn to meditate. I will never forget the intense challenge of those early days, sitting on my couch trying to quiet my mind. It was excruciating; and I quickly started seeking meditation teachers and practices to help me find peace in the midst of the chaos of early recovery.

In those tender days and months of learning how to let myself feel without numbing through drugs and alcohol, I began to learn about my breath. One of my favorite breath-focused meditation practices was to simply count 1-2-3-4 on the inhale and 4-3-2-1 on the exhale. This was the only thing that helped my mind settle, even for a few seconds. And it was in those seconds that I eventually started the very lengthy process of learning how to regulate my emotions without the need for substances.

When I got out of rehab I went back to college to study printmaking, and after graduating I moved to San Francisco to pursue an MFA in socially engaged art. After graduate school I began teaching art and traveling for exhibitions and lectures. While I was living as an artist, I kept up with my breathing and meditation practices, albeit in a very imperfect way. I would have months of rigorous practice followed by months of no practice at all. It took me years to learn to be consistent despite the suggestions from my teachers and nearly every book I read on meditation. In my late twenties, I began to develop a deeper practice of simply breathing and being with myself. And that's when my life and spiritual development accelerated in tremendous ways.

During those intense years of personal discovery and study, I found myself drawn to different schools of Buddhism and various branches of Hatha yoga, and I eventually found my way into studying energy medicine, medical intuition, neuroscience, and somatic psychotherapy.

While living in Berlin on a grant from the Danish Arts Council, I created a blog about how I was changing my life through meditation, yoga, and eating whole foods. I started the project as a way to process and understand my own transition, but within six months I had friends asking me to coach them through their own lifestyle struggles; I realized my struggles were not unique and that the tools I was using could be made available to anyone. Before I knew it, I felt the call to move to Los Angeles and start a holistic health practice.

I arrived in Los Angeles with one friend and a big dream of supporting people in their work to inhabit their bodies. At the time I didn't know exactly how it would unfold, but for the first time in what seemed like forever, I knew I was where I was supposed to be. I jumped into a yoga teacher training course with one of my dearest teachers, Tony Giuliano, and after completing it I began teaching in studios across the city. Within a year I realized that I was less interested in teaching asana (yoga postures) and more interested in teaching about the breath.

What I loved about the breath was that it was more accessible than yoga poses and traditional meditation practices. It felt really modern and fresh to me, despite the fact that many breathing practices had been around for thousands of years. What I also loved about the breath was that it was a very direct way to work with my body while also working with my emotions and spirit. It was the ultimate integrative remedy.

I decided to take the plunge and scale down my offerings to focus solely on the deeper aspects of breathwork after studying the breath with a few other teachers from various backgrounds. Narrowing the scope of my practice was one of the smartest personal and business decisions I've ever made. It allowed me to dive much deeper than I could go while juggling so many aspects of my previous holistic health practice. I also recognized that, if I wanted to become an expert in this space, I would have to devote more of my time and energy to it. The beauty of this work is that there is always more to learn, and narrowing in gave me room to expand into the depths of what is possible with the breath.

As my teaching and client practice grew, I began developing my own unique breathing practices for clients born out of their specific needs. Many of my clients didn't relate to the language or mythology around more classical breath practices. I realized that breathwork as a healing technology needed a major update to make it accessible in the modern world. From getting a better night's sleep, to reducing anxiety, to setting boundaries, the practices in *How to Breathe* will help you develop a consistent practice of being with yourself.

Being a full-time breathwork teacher for the last several years, and creating my own practices and methodology for working with the breath, has given me the courage to take the next step in my growth and write this book. Truth be told, I wrote my first book in elementary school and have had an affinity for the power books have to change our lives since my days of winning summer reading contests at the local library.

People often ask me why I teach breathwork and what breathwork means to me. While there are many reasons, all of which you will discover as you read the pages of this book, it really comes down to a desire to fully inhabit my body, and my passion for supporting others to do the same. I spent so many years of my life disassociating, checking out, and numbing (even after I stopped drinking and using drugs) that I realized my deepest desire was to feel present within myself, to feel anchored to the earth, to be able to self-regulate, and to know deeply that I had the ability to trust my inner wisdom. After years of creating safe spaces for my clients to explore their breath and bodies and all that comes with it, I want to share with you the practices that are changing our lives.

This book will introduce you to the foundations of breathwork and my methodology. It outlines the scientific-supported benefits; explains how the breath relates to emotions, the stress response, and resilience; and presents the best ways to engage in breathwork. From there, you will discover twenty-five breathing practices for everyday situations that are easy to integrate into modern life, including breathwork for anxiety, relaxation, energy, and more. Each practice features an introduction explaining the origin, benefits, and purpose of the breathwork, followed by step-by-step instructions and post practice notes.

the Foundational Tool

Breath is the foundation for many healing arts practices, including meditation, yoga, and energetic medicine. Becoming curious about your breath is the quickest way to shift your emotions, thoughts, and vibration. In this section, I share the most essential things you need to know about breathing, the anatomy of breath, and how the breath and emotions are inextricably linked.

THE UNIVERSAL BREATH

At a very basic level breath is the foundation for life. A general rule of thumb is that humans can go for about three weeks without food, three days without water, and three minutes without oxygen. Not only is our breath essential to keeping us alive, it is also the key practice for modern-day wellness. It is beneficial to our overall health, resilience, and personal and collective growth.

Throughout history breath has often been associated with the concept of a life force or spirit. Interestingly, this connection is apparent in many corners of the world, across many cultures and disciplines. In Greek, the word *psyche* can be translated as "life" or "breath." In Latin, the word *spiritus* means "breath" and is also where we derive the modern-day word *spirit*. The Sanskrit word *pranayama* comes from the words *prana* (life energy) and *ayama* (to extend, draw out). In classical Hatha yoga, pranayama is the practice of regulating the breath through techniques for specific health benefits.

There are tai chi breathing practices specifically designed to strengthen the diaphragm and acupuncture points in Chinese medicine to open the flow of qi (or life force) in the body. In some African and South American traditions, the breath is used to release spirits from the body, thus aiding in the healing of the individual and the community.

In addition to the rich historical landscape of the breath, we are learning today through neuroscience research that a number of nerve cells in the brain stem connect breathing to different states of mind. This research is significant because it confirms what thinkers, healers, and mystics have known for ages: we have the power to shift our thinking by changing the way we breathe. And since it's already common knowledge that our thoughts affect our overall health, energy, and well-being, it's safe to conclude that changing our breathing can have a global effect on our entire body.

A BASIC ANATOMY OF BREATHING

Our respiratory system is responsible for taking in oxygen and releasing carbon dioxide. Adults typically breathe twelve to twenty breaths per minute, which is about 20,000 cycles every 24 hours. This rate increases with physical exertion and decreases while in a resting state. Just to give you an idea of how the body uses oxygen, about 25 percent of it is used by the brain, while the kidneys use 12 percent and the heart just 7 percent. Our bodies need oxygen to sustain themselves and need to be able to expel carbon dioxide to cleanse the system. Breath is a natural detoxifier. When we think of cleansing these days, the go-to usually has something to do with the food we eat. And while that is essential for wellness, making sure we are breathing well throughout the day is an impactful way to keep our system clean and clear.

The major body parts and organs that are involved with breathing are the mouth, nose, larynx (voice box), trachea, lungs, and diaphragm. When we breathe, oxygen enters the nose or mouth. The air moves through the pharynx (throat), larynx, and trachea into the lungs. Then air is exhaled, flowing back through the same pathway. One of the reasons I encourage my clients to breathe through their nose (when they are not engaged in strenuous exercise) is because inhaling through the nose enhances endurance and increases our ability to focus. The nose is also a defense against bacteria and produces nitric oxide, which is a very important compound for cardiovascular, immune, and sexual health.

Once the air is in the body, it flows through the trachea (windpipe) and then moves to the bronchi, two tubes that carry air into each lung. From there it goes into the lungs, where the oxygen is exchanged for carbon dioxide. The bloodstream delivers oxygen to cells and removes waste, or carbon dioxide, through internal respiration. During exhalation, air passes from the lungs through the larynx and then out the nose or mouth.

When I teach first-time clients or a breathwork basics class, I tend to spend most of my time on the diaphragm because it is the primary breathing muscle, and it's a part of the body that most of us aren't very familiar with.

The diaphragm is a very deep muscle, with an asymmetrical double-domed shape located at the base of the chest that divides the torso into the thoracic and abdominal cavities (or sections).

Access Your Diaphragm

Take your hands and place one at each side of your torso, with fingers facing forward and your pinky fingers touching your bottom ribs. Breathe gently in and out through your nose. Feel your sides expand on the inhale and release on the exhale to get a sense of how your diaphragm is working inside your body with each breath.

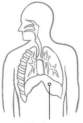

diaphragm

During normal inhalation, the diaphragm contracts and moves downward, which increases the space in your chest, giving your lungs room to expand. When you exhale, the diaphragm releases and moves upward and your lungs return to their neutral position. Because of the deeply domed shape of the diaphragm, I often tell students to watch jellyfish videos online to get a visual sense of how the diaphragm moves in our body while we breathe. There is something quite ethereal about those sea creatures that gives a very sensory experience of how our diaphragm contracts and expands.

One more thing of note about the diaphragm is that its shape is created by the organs enclosing and surrounding it, like the liver and heart. These relationships and the interconnectedness of these organs are essential to consider when working with other systems in the body.

BREATH AND THE STRESS RESPONSE

It's impossible to explore the breath without looking at the autonomic nervous system (ANS). The ANS connects the brain to the body and is a two-way street. If you're anxious or stressed by an event in your life or from thinking about an event, the brain, via the nerves of the ANS, will most likely turn on the sympathetic part of that system (your fight-or-flight response).

When you are in a calm or relaxed state, your ANS will turn on the parasympathetic part of the system (your rest-and-digest mode).

Rest and Digest versus Fight or Flight

Most of us have heard of "fight or flight," but not as many have heard of "rest and digest." These are the two sides of the coin when it comes to your autonomic nervous system. When under stress, the sympathetic part of your system turns on, increasing heart rate and blood pressure, preparing you to deal with the challenge ahead. When relaxed and calm, the parasympathetic part of the system is engaged; your heart rate comes down, your blood pressure lowers, and your breathing slows.

During inhalation, the heart gets stimulated to beat a little faster. During the following exhale, the heart gets a message to slow down. The overall effect is very little change in the heart rate from minute to minute. However, when you make one part of the breath cycle, either the inhale or the exhale, longer than the other, and you do this for several minutes, the accumulated effect is that you will either slow your heart rate down or speed it up, depending on where you began.

When you extend your exhale by one to two counts longer than your inhale and you practice this for a couple of minutes, your heart rate will slow down. This sends a feedback message to the brain saying that everything is more peaceful and calm than it was a few minutes ago. This lets the brain support this shift further by turning on the rest and-digest mode of the nervous system, which goes back from the brain to the body. The amazing thing is that the lungs and heart can send feedback to the brain and essentially convince the brain that things are calm and peaceful, even when there are still stressful circumstances or anxiety-provoking thoughts circulating in the mind.

This is especially important in modern life, when internal and external stressors are often constant even though we are in no physical danger. I often hear from clients that they are stressed about the never-ending stream of email in their in-boxes and the feeling of having to check their phones first thing in the morning. In some people, anxiety or stress can cause a freeze response, which is typically marked by a fast and short inhale that is held until the body has to release the carbon dioxide. After our first session, they often report holding their breath while glancing over email on their phones.

This type of breath response can reinforce the physical feeling of stress. This is one example of how our systems are becoming increasingly taxed and overloaded in our modern world and how stress can perpetuate itself. Breathwork is an excellent practice to stop that cycle in its tracks. Anxiety and stress cannot live in the body if you consciously slow down your breathing, because they require a cycle of fast and shallow breathing.

The majority of the breathing exercises in the Breathwork Practices section of this book are designed to strengthen your parasympathetic nervous system (PNS) to help you move easily into conscious healing as well as grounded and restful states. Over the years of working with clients and teaching groups, I've found that the majority of the people I work with don't need their sympathetic systems turned on any higher, so the focus is less on getting them super energized and more on how to ground and replenish their systems. For those of you who are looking for more energizing practices, I have included a couple of them for you as well.

THE POWER OF THE EXHALE

One of my main areas of focus with new clients is on the exhale. Since the vast majority of the people I work with have a tendency to either hold their breath, have very short exhales, or feel challenged by exhaling, I have found that is a good place to begin to explore the breath. I also hone in on this area because, as I mentioned before, the exhale correlates with the parasympathetic nervous system (our rest-and-digest mode), which is a system that usually needs support.

One thing I've seen consistently over the years is that many of the people I work with are either entirely on or entirely off, with no balance in between (this can also be a marker of trauma, which I touch on a little later in this section). They have no idea how to truly rest, and they don't have a practice of rest that is actually nourishing and restorative. For many, rest tends to look like numbing, checking out, avoiding, or suppressing. This might sound surprising, but it's much more common than most of us realize.

Take a moment to contemplate the last time you felt relaxed, restored, or deeply replenished. If that was recently, congrats; you're on the right track. If you can't remember the last time you felt that way or it was really long ago, don't worry; this book will serve as a guide to help you ground your system and process what's coming up along the way, and to give you accessible practices to help you learn to take deeper care of yourself.

A big part of the issue is that our world is moving at lightning speed. With so many demands on our energy and time, it is no wonder most of us feel burned out and depleted at some point or another. For me, running a full-time practice, writing, being in a relationship, planning for a family, taking care of myself, and making sure to see my loved ones requires me to function at a very high level most of the time. For those of you who are also full of passion and energy for the work that you do, it can be challenging to hit the pause button and reset. I've learned the hard way over many years of trial and epic errors that working with my exhale has ultimately been incredibly rewarding albeit very challenging at times. It has led to a deeply spiritual journey of learning how to listen to my body and move at a pace that is comfortable for it, rather than getting caught up in the speed of my mind or world around me.

With patience, time, and practice, nearly everyone I have worked with has developed a new relationship to their exhale, and it has proven time and time again to be a real turning point in people's lives. The power of the exhale lives in the invitation to slow down with presence, which is completely different than checking out, suppressing, or numbing. The power of the exhale lives in our bodies' inherent wisdom that we need to hit the pause and refresh button on ourselves just as much (and I'd argue even more) as we do on all of our technology. The power of the exhale not only helps us reduce anxiety and find our ground but also supports a wider range of resilience, which opens us up to a world of possibilities for our health and well-being.

BREATH AND EMOTIONS

Just for fun, try holding your breath for a minute while feeling joyful. Challenging, isn't it? Breath is directly connected to the amount of spaciousness or freedom we feel in our bodies; without it, we feel constricted. This affects our capacity to tolerate intense and pleasant emotions and experiences. Our window of tolerance correlates to our breath, and if we breathe with ease, depth, fullness, and flow, all aspects of life can feel more expansive.

Imagine just for a moment being frustrated. As you imagine being frustrated, notice how your breath begins to shift. You might experience it being shorter, constricted, or caught in your chest. Now imagine yourself feeling grateful and notice how your breath changes yet again. In this simple example, it's easy to see just how connected our breath and emotions are.

The quality and intensity of our emotions, either positive or negative, is connected to how we breathe. If our breathing pattern tends to be on the restrictive side, that often correlates with a tendency to check out or suppress difficult emotions. Restrictive and stagnant breathing patterns are often previous attempts to cope with emotional or physical events that can go as far back as when we were in utero. On the flip side, if our breath tends to be more spacious and fluid, this relates to the openness and ease we feel in our body and with self-expression.

When we are afraid to share how we feel or lack the skills to articulate what is happening for us, these feelings are consciously repressed or subconsciously suppressed. These repressed and suppressed feelings end up being stored in the body and over time manifest as chronic tension, pain, and eventually disease. The magic of learning to work with the breath is that we all have the built-in equipment we need to learn how to change our feelings (energy) and transform how they are expressed in our bodies.

Before ending this subsection on breath and emotions, I have to talk about the diaphragm again. In more esoteric terms, the diaphragm is said to separate heaven and earth as it crosses the solar plexus, an area associated with the spleen in Chinese medicine that relates to personal power, self-esteem, and self-discipline. Given its shape, location, and function in the body, I often describe the diaphragm as a lid containing emotions and experiences that we have repressed or suppressed in the body. This is one of the main reasons some forms of breathwork are associated with deep emotional healing. When you start to pay attention to your diaphragm and work with it through the breath, you process emotions somatically, or in the body, as opposed to processing them through the cognitive mind, as is common in the majority of psychotherapy practices.

BREATH AND ANXIETY

If bringing awareness to the breath creates anxiety, it's often connected to a dysregulated nervous system. This dysregulation has a major impact on the breath. When I work with clients who have this experience, we begin by exploring their nervous system and creating the container for it to come into a more regulated state. To do this, I start with the outer edges of the body, such as bringing awareness to the feet, and slowly work inward to allow an easier way for clients to ground themselves. As regulation takes shape, their breath tends to naturally, and without effort, become less anxious. In this more relaxed state, it is then safe to move into targeted breathwork practices.

BREATH AND TRAUMA

The experience of being overwhelmed by thoughts and emotions is often a marker of trauma. Trauma is anything that we experience as a threat to our survival or overall well-being. These threats register in our nervous system, and if the natural restoration process is interrupted, coping mechanisms are put in place to survive the experiences. If left unprocessed, those coping mechanisms may lead to belief and behavioral changes that create patterns that are difficult to heal without addressing the body, the nervous system, and the breath.

Breathwork is incredibly powerful because, with proper pacing and guidance, it can be an entry point into the nervous system. This has the potential, along with body-focused counseling, to help restore the nervous system's natural rhythm. When this system is reestablished, the client is no longer in a trauma response cycle and the root of the trauma can be healed.

When I started teaching breathwork, I often taught very activating practices in big groups. As the size of my classes increased, I began noticing there were always a handful of students who got flooded with memories and stored emotions; they couldn't cope with the practice because their nervous system didn't have the capacity to handle their experiences. I started working with those students privately and learned that the activating breathwork practices opened them up too fast, which is why their systems went into overload. These clients needed a different approach to working with their breath.

Knowing that the breath can be a key component in trauma healing, I set out to deepen my personal practice and studies; I researched cutting-edge psychology, somatic therapies, and neuroscience, which shifted my approach to the breath as it relates to developmental and relational trauma. While working with clients privately and in groups, I developed my own set of practices and methodology that continues to support my clients, allowing them to shift the root of their trauma and integrate their past with their present. These practices are outside the scope of this book and are taught in my individual sessions and classes.

Create *a* Practice

It's easy to get overwhelmed with how to start a practice when you're busy, have a family, or are new to self-care and establishing time for yourself. In this section, I guide you through my go-to best methods for establishing a breathwork practice and staying consistent

INTENTION IS EVERYTHING

Intentions give you purpose and direction, and serve as a touchstone when developing a personal breathwork practice. If we don't tap into our motivation to connect to our breath on a regular basis, it's easy to get lost and forget why we started a breathwork practice in the first place.

Intentions are different than goals, as they are less focused on outcomes and more about the driving force that's supporting your journey. An intention is like the North Star, a guiding energy that will bring you back home to yourself again and again. Without this aim and reference guide, our practice sessions can feel uncontained and unstable.

Setting an intention at the beginning of your breathwork practice sets the tone for it and keeps you connected to why you are practicing. This becomes key when things get tough in your life or in your practice, as they inevitably will from time to time. It's also important because many of my clients have reported that when their lives get really great and full, their practice starts to wane.

No matter the length of my personal breathwork sessions, I always make sure to set an intention. I have a very simple intention-setting practice of placing one hand on my heart, taking a couple of breaths in and out through my nose, and trusting the first intuitive hit I receive about my intention for that practice session.

When setting your intention, it's important to keep it affirmative, clear, and focused on your internal well-being or personal and spiritual growth. There are many intention practices out there for manifesting tangible things like houses, careers, and relationships, but for the purposes of setting your intention before breathwork, it's most potent to focus on your personal, internal desires.

Here are some examples:

> *I intend to stay in my body.*
>
> *I intend to receive myself fully.*
>
> *I intend to stay with the practice.*
>
> *I intend to soften.*
>
> *I intend to follow my breath.*
>
> *I intend to open my heart.*
>
> *I intend to hold a strong container for myself.*

I intend to feel what's calling to be felt.

I intend to heal myself.

Once you have identified your intention, say it silently to yourself or aloud before you begin your practice session. You can use your intention throughout your practice as a foundational guide to help you stay connected to your practice. At the end of your session, it can be helpful to journal about your intention in your notes as a way to further integrate the intention.

PRIORITIZING YOURSELF

If there is one consistent issue that many of my clients bring to their first sessions with me, aside from anxiety and stress, it is not knowing how to prioritize themselves. This has been a huge theme in so many lives, myself included, and starting a breathwork practice can be a wonderful, tangible way to take one step toward putting yourself first.

By the time this book makes it into your hands, I'll be a mother, which I already know will change my entire life. Not only will it help me grow and expand to new lengths, it will also challenge the work I've been doing on myself for the last sixteen years around my own self-care and learning how to put myself before others. Thankfully, I have been supporting parents in my practice for years and have learned from their bravery, honesty, and vulnerability some of what it takes to show up for your family without losing yourself.

Regardless of whether we want to have children or not, there is always some project or person that needs our attention. Many of us have been socialized to take care of others' needs before our own. As a result, we have kept ourselves small, not spoken up about our feelings or needs, and learned to shift ourselves to make others feel okay. What's amazing about taking this step toward developing your own breathwork practice is that you not only get all the benefits of the practice itself but also engage in a revolutionary act that affirms that your needs matter.

THE MOST EFFECTIVE POSTURES AND WHERE THEY WORK BEST

There are three postures that I recommend for breathwork: sitting up, standing, and lying down. In the Breathwork Practices section of this book, I discuss which posture is ideal for each practice.

Sitting up

Sitting up is the most common posture for meditation, and it's great for breathwork as well. While seated practices are usually taught seated on the floor with legs crossed, I have found that sitting on a chair with feet firmly planted on the floor is the most ideal posture for a seated breathwork practice. This is especially true if you have tight hips, have difficulty sitting on the floor, or tend to feel ungrounded in your life. If you fall into one or more of these three categories, begin by sitting in a chair. If you're an experienced meditator or yogi and prefer to sit directly on the floor or on a meditation bench or yoga block, please feel free.

IN A CHAIR: Sit in a chair that has a firm seat and back. If you require extra support, place a pillow behind your low back so that your spine can be tall. Notice if your head is leaning forward, and if so, draw it back to align just over your shoulders. This takes extra weight off your spine and makes it easier to sit up tall. Place your feet on the floor hip distance apart. Let your arms rest on your thighs, palms of the hands down if you're cold and up if you're warm. Alternatively, you can rest one hand on top of the other on your lap, palms facing up.

ON THE FLOOR: Sit directly on the floor or on a meditation cushion with legs crossed. Notice if your head is leaning forward, and if so, draw it back to align just over your shoulders. Rest your hands on your knees, palms face down if you're cold and up if you're warm.

Alternatively, you can rest one hand on top of the other on your lap, palms facing up. Another option for the floor is to sit on a meditation bench or yoga block. Kneel on the ground and place the bench or block just under your bottom. Sit up tall and lengthen your spine. Notice if your head is leaning forward, and if so, draw it back to align just over your shoulders. Rest your hands on your knees, palms face down if you're cold and up if you're warm. Alternatively, you can rest one hand on top of the other on your lap, palms facing up.

Standing up

The standing posture is the least taught in breathwork but one that I find essential for certain practices, especially those around grounding or moving intense energy. This posture is very simple and is best done with shoes and socks off so that you can feel the connection to the floor or earth.

Stand up tall with your feet hip width apart. Notice if your head is leaning forward, and if so, draw it back to align just over your shoulders. Let your arms rest by your sides slightly turned out with your palms facing forward.

Lying down

Lying on your back is an ideal posture for restorative breathwork practices as well as practices where you are moving sadness or grief, tapping into intuition, or addressing sleep. There are two ways to practice lying down, with or without neck and low back support.

To practice without support, simply lie down on the floor, preferably on a mat or blanket so you are comfortable. Rest your arms down by your sides or have one hand on your belly and one on your heart. To practice with support, lie down and place a soft pillow or rolled up blanket under your knees to support the low back and something similar under your neck. Rest your arms down by your sides or have one hand on your belly and one on your heart.

THE RITUAL OF HOME PRACTICE

A yoga teacher once told me that thirty minutes of home practice was the equivalent of a ninety-minute class. That stuck with me because it made so much sense. Cultivating a home practice is one of the best things you can do for your self-care and development. It's not easy, but believe me, it's worth it.

The first aspect of home practice is setting up your space. For some of my clients, this means a room or corner of a room that is their dedicated practice space. Others practice in their bedroom. They do it seated at the edge of their beds, lying down in bed, or in a chair in the room. The purpose of a dedicated practice space is that over time that particular place comes to hold a certain energy that your body immediately connects to when you begin your practice. It's also a nod to creating ritual around your practice, which is a key component that infuses your practice with meaning and a loose structure of support.

Take a tour of your home with the intention of choosing a place to practice each day. If you're not sure where to begin, just pick a place and practice in it for a week. Don't stress about this part: the important thing is to choose and begin; you can always pick a different place later.

When you decide where you are going to practice, put an offering in that area that feels supportive to your practice. It can be a piece of artwork, a crystal, a feather, a flower, or a photograph of a teacher you admire. Think of this as the beginning of your altar, or place that holds your offerings. If you have time and interest, you can add several offerings to your altar. If only one offering feels right, that's great too. The point of the offering is to choose something that helps you drop into your practice and supports your overall intentions.

Lastly, if there are things you need for your practice, like a blanket, cushion, or journal, be sure those items are in your practice area. I find that having those items in a specific place along with your offerings sets up a wonderful invitation to practice. The idea is to make the space, whether it's an entire room or the corner of a shared area, a place where you want to practice. I have a few singing bowls set up in my space that are always encouraging me to play them; this makes it much easier for me to practice some days.

LETTING GO OF HOW IT'S SUPPOSED TO LOOK

While it's important to set an intention and have a dedicated practice space, we have to be willing to let all of that go in an instant. The dog is barking at the door and there is an unexpected delivery we have to tend to. A child comes in to talk to us. We're on vacation and would rather practice on the beach (by all means do!). We're too tired to get to the other room, and we decide to do our breathwork practice in bed, lying down in the morning. We go to our dedicated practice space and realize we're just too hungry and need to make a snack instead.

No matter what's happening in our lives around our home practice, it's important to have a judgment-free practice. This can be challenging, especially with how inundated we are with imagery of people being "healthy" and "spiritual" all over social media and the internet. It can feel like we're doing it wrong because our practice looks really messy and inconsistent sometimes, or more often than we care to admit!

You're okay and your practice is too. The most generous gift we can give to ourselves is to drop the judgment and shame around our practice and simply do what we can each day. As someone who suffered from brutal self judgment and shame most of my life, I can tell you that softening up and allowing myself to color outside the lines, so to speak, in my breathwork practice and other areas of my life has opened me up to such immense freedom and lightness in my heart.

THE MYTH OF NEEDING TO PRACTICE IN SILENCE

It can be annoying to hear a lot of noise while you're trying to find your zen, but it's part of life and we need to learn to adjust to it. I remember ages ago being on a silent meditation retreat and on day three wanting to crawl out of my skin because I felt like the man next to me was breathing too loudly. I literally felt like I was going insane, and I was convinced he was ruining my retreat experience. When I think about it now I laugh, but at the time it was incredibly aggravating.

One tip I learned early on was any outside sound that bothers you is simply an invitation to anchor yourself back in your breath and in your body. The beauty of a breathwork practice is you have an actual noise machine with you, your breath, that you can change the volume on if needed to support your mind to settle during your practice. If you're sensitive to outside sounds, I suggest breathing a little bit louder to help you ground into your practice and stay in your body.

PORTABLE PRACTICE

One of my favorite aspects of breathwork is that it is portable. You don't need a special outfit or props to practice; you have everything you need to begin with you at all times.

Early on in my private practice clients asked me for tips on what they could do breathwork-wise to support them outside of our sessions and their personal practices. Below are three of my go-to mini practices to support those real-life moments when you need to stay grounded.

If you tend to get stressed at work, feel anxious preparing for difficult conversations, or feel out of your body before getting in front of a large crowd, try the Five-Breath Grounding Practice.

Set a quick intention. Place your feet on the ground, hip distance apart, and take five deep breaths in through your nose and long exhales out of your mouth. Notice how you feel afterward.

When you feel emotionally or mentally overloaded and need a quick time-out, try the Five-Breath Reset Practice.

Set a quick intention. Inhale through your nose as long as you can without discomfort, then exhale as long as possible through your mouth. Repeat five times and notice the difference.

If your mind is racing and you can't get it to focus on the present moment, try the Five-Breath Alignment Practice.

Set a quick intention. Take a deep inhale through your nose while counting from 1 to 5. Exhale through your nose while counting from 5 to 1. Repeat this five times and become aware of where your mind lands.

NATURE IS A HUGE HELPER

When possible, practice your breathwork in nature. This is an incredible way to connect to the elements and the earth, which further regulates your nervous system and deepens your breathwork practice experience. Some of the most profound breathwork sessions I've had personally have been outside either in the woods or near the beach. Syncing up with the rhythms and cycles of nature through our breath is incredibly replenishing and restorative to our well-being on all levels.

Two of my favorite ways to practice in nature are with my back against a tree, which immediately anchors my body, or lying on the natural ground, the grass or a sandy beach.

TRACKING YOUR PRACTICE: JOURNALING

Journaling is an ideal way to track your practice, keep notes on what you're discovering, and be able to see how far you have come over time. Creating a dedicated breathwork journal and writing down a few sentences about each practice session deepens your personal work and creates richer practice experiences.

There are many ways to record information these days, and while I am a fan of using note apps and voice notes, the act of writing helps the brain and body sync up, which helps you to integrate what you're learning in your sessions.

Keep it simple with the journal. After your breathwork session at home, write down a few sentences or notes about your experience, what came up, something new that you learned or felt, a creative idea that popped up, an intuitive hit you received, a pattern that you recognized, or a new layer of work that you want to explore.

Sometimes in sessions so much comes up that it can be tempting to stop the session to write things down. Over the years I've learned that it's better to keep the flow of the session going and to trust that if you're meant to remember it, you will at the end.

If your journal is portable, it can be great to take it with you when you leave the house so that you can track what's happening with your breath throughout the day. Some of the practices in this book are meant to be done on the spot, and if your journal is handy you can keep track of what's working well for you.

CONSISTENCY IS EVERYTHING

Just like my saying the way we breathe is how we live, the way we practice is also how we live. No matter what teacher or expert I speak to in any field, what I hear repeatedly is that if you want to build a practice, you have to be consistent.

The twenty-minute meditation is very popular in the wellness world for many reasons, including accessing different brain wave states. While this time frame works for some people in some schools of meditation, it doesn't really apply to breathwork because our practice by nature is more active and somatically focused.

When I learned to meditate, I started with five minutes. When I learned to practice breathwork, I began with seven minutes. For the practices in this book, I suggest specific lengths of time as a starting point to the particular practice. Some are designed to be quick and others are designed to go longer. If you are new to breathwork, please use the times as a guide and adjust them as needed.

The main point I want to stress about consistency is that it is not about the length of time that you practice; rather, it's about practicing as often as possible. Anytime you want to learn something new you practice. Our nervous systems are built on repetition; this is how we learn.

I've heard so many people say, "Oh I tried breathwork and nothing changed" or "I tried meditation and it didn't work." When I inquire a little more, they usually say they tried for a day or two and they didn't receive the desired or promised benefit. Imagine you wanted to learn to play the piano and you had never played an instrument and didn't know how to read music. Picture yourself at your first lesson. Would you leave thinking, "Oh, piano isn't for me, I can't play?" Maybe. Or perhaps you would recognize that it's going to take time and dedication to be able to read music and make beautiful sounds.

The thing is, most of us haven't spent that much time paying attention to our breath or living in our bodies, so it can feel really weird to start a breathwork practice. In the beginning, it can be very challenging just to be with ourselves, no distractions, just us and our breath and the body that we have been running from for so long.

If you want to develop a relationship to your breath and ultimately to your life force and spirit, you are going to have to be in this for the long haul. I realize that might sound daunting, given that this book is for beginners, but it's the truth. Exploring our breath is the start of a lifetime journey of learning, one inhale and exhale at a time, to inhabit our bodies and live from a place of fullness and presence.

ESTABLISHING A PRACTICE

Being dedicated and devoted to your practice is essential. Before you begin the practices in the next section, spend some time thinking about why you want to practice breathwork. What is drawing you to this modality? Why are you interested in this work? When you are clear on your why, it's much easier to commit to practicing each day, imperfectly of course, with attention, care, and love.

How you practice depends on your home and work life. For some of my clients, it means having their partner take care of the kids for an allotted amount of practice time each day; for others, it looks like getting it in their calendars and setting a reminder alert; and for others, it looks like practicing away from home in the office before or after work. Set aside some time to think about what adding a breathwork practice to your day might look like and where it would feel best in your current schedule, and be willing to experiment with different approaches until you find what works best for you.

I suggest that you practice daily, and when I say that, I mean it with as much softness and spaciousness as possible. You don't want your breathwork practice to be one more thing on your never-ending to-do list. Instead, frame your breathwork practice as your time each day to do a deeper level of self-care by getting in touch with your life energy, your emotions, and your body.

In the beginning, it's preferable to practice around the same time each day. This helps reinforce our nervous systems, which learn through repetition, and sets up our body to know, just like we know when we're hungry or need to stretch, that it's time to practice. With time and dedication, your body and mind will come to look forward to your breathwork practice as a time to nourish yourself, gain clarity, and center yourself in the here and now.

For those of you who work for yourselves or have busy family lives with ever-changing schedules, practice each day when you can. You will still receive the benefits of the practice and, again, the real key is to get it in each day just like you do your veggies and water. It's more important to practice than it is to feel like your practice has to look a certain way.

If you already have a meditation practice, you can add one of the breathwork practices to it. If all of this is new to you, then start by choosing a practice in the next section that resonates with you in that moment. For those who are new to establishing a practice, I recommend starting with one practice and doing it every day for two weeks. At the end of those weeks, evaluate where you are and continue with that practice or choose a different one for the next two weeks.

CLOSING YOUR PRACTICE

At the end of most of the practices in the next section I have a note about closing your practice. Taking a few moments to acknowledge the end of your practice will help you assimilate what you gained from your session. It is also an easy way to transition into your next activity feeling more aware.

In many yoga classes it is common to come out of savasana into a seated meditation, placing your hands together in front of your heart and recognizing the teacher within. I find this to be a grounding way to support and affirm my focus from class, allowing it to linger throughout the day. Gently coming out of your breathwork practice by closing it has a similar effect and gives you an opportunity to shift into whatever is next with ease.

I suggest keeping your closing direct and uncomplicated. A brief internal or vocal acknowledgement that your practice time has ended is sufficient. If you want to take the closing a step further, revisit your intention from the beginning of your practice and re-affirm it silently or aloud.

You will find that some of the shorter practices in the next section don't lend themselves to long closings, and a few practices don't have any closing instructions. Experiment with closing the shorter practices in a way that feels good to you. Often a quick acknowledgement that the practice is over is plenty to move forward.

25 Breathwork Practices

In the following pages, you will discover twenty-five breathwork practices that are easy to integrate into modern life. From getting a better night's sleep, to reducing anxiety, to setting boundaries, the breathing practices in this section are the most effective tools I've created for establishing a sense of connection, relief, and deeper purpose in every aspect of life. The practices are presented in alphabetical order. Each one has a simple title followed by an in-depth explanation of its benefits, the specific breathwork instructions, and notes that shed light on the nuances of each practice.

Breathwork can be practiced with eyes open or closed depending on your comfort level. Closing the eyes pulls our attention inward, removing external visual distractions. This can help quiet the mind, supporting a deeper level of attunement to the breath, body, and internal landscape. Practicing with the eyes open is helpful if you want to stay visually oriented to the world around you, bring energy into your practice, or aren't ready to fully go inward. This is useful if you are just starting a breathwork practice or don't feel safe in your body. It's important to acknowledge your needs and allow your eyes to support you in the best way. This will open up more possibility for your breathwork practice to have greater benefits.

Anger

Anger is a natural and often unwanted emotion that can be very difficult to express. Anger can arise from a wide range of experiences, like a long commute in traffic, being treated unfairly, not being heard, or being criticized at work or by a loved one. How we experience anger can range from a mild irritation to intense frustration to fiery rage. While experiencing anger is part of the human experience, it's important to have a tool for cooling the flames and taking a closer look at what anger is trying to tell us.

Most psychologists agree that anger is a secondary emotion, meaning it is fueled by primary emotions like fear or sadness. Fear and sadness are two of the most challenging emotions to face, as they require us to confront our own vulnerability and the reality of life's uncertainty. To avoid being seen as or feeling too vulnerable, anger comes online to help us feel like we're running the show and have more power in and over our lives.

Let's face it, we all get angry, and there are few places where it's acceptable to express our anger. Because of that, it's usually one of the first emotions to get stuffed down and stored in our bodies. I've heard many of my clients say, too many times to count, that they "never get angry." After a few sessions together, they become aware that they do in fact get angry, but they have just been afraid to feel it. This is largely because we live in a culture that tells us anger is a negative emotion, that it should be avoided at all costs, and if for some reason you do express anger, you are labeled as aggressive, hostile, or worse.

The Anger Breath is a calming aid that helps regulate the nervous system and shift us from an activated flight-or-flight response to a grounded place of case. Anger is often accompanied by a short, staccato breath that is shallow in the chest. These physiological markers are indicators that our sympathetic nervous system is switched on. You've probably been advised, "Count backward from 10 to 1" to reduce anger, and while there is some truth to that, switching up your breath is a much faster way to change your state and create a different experience. When we're able to downshift our anger with the breath, it's easier to feel into the primary emotions just underneath the anger, see the larger picture, and facilitate mindful action. The Anger Breath is also a helpful tool for putting our attention on what we have control over instead of wasting our energy on what isn't ours to control.

Anger

THE PRACTICE

Stand with your feet hip distance apart.

Set an intention for your practice.

Take long breaths in through your nose.

Exhale quickly through your mouth.

Repeat this for three rounds.

Place one of your hands on your belly.

Inhale deeply through your nose.

Exhale gently through your nose.

As you breathe, bring your attention to your hand, observing the natural rise and fall of your belly.

Repeat this for two full minutes.

Close your practice.

Note any changes you experienced.

Journal.

This is a very simple and effective practice for bringing an activated nervous system into a grounded, more relaxed state. The Anger Breath is meant to serve as a tool to shift you out of the immediate, pressing anger you are experiencing, and it can be used to clear past hurts as well. Breathing with your hand on your belly is an effective way to guide your body to where you want to be breathing. Over time and with practice your body builds a somatic memory of having your hand on your belly when you're regulating anger, and it will begin to shift your breath without much effort. This is one of the ways that our bodies are incredibly brilliant and efficient in an effort to bring us to a state of calm, health, and overall well-being.

Anger has such a stigma in the wellness community, which undermines and negates our humanness and makes it easy to feel that if we experience anger we are doing something wrong and aren't healthy. Instead of looking at anger as the enemy, I guide my clients toward viewing their anger as an internal alarm that is letting them know something isn't right. With this shift in perspective we can let anger be our teacher, leading us into the places we've been avoiding within ourselves, guiding us to stand up for the injustices that are against our values, and reminding us with every breath that we are spiritual beings having a human experience.

Boundaries

One of the most healthy habits we can learn is to have clear and strong boundaries. Early on I learned that we set boundaries for ourselves, not for others, and that boundaries are not selfish; they are a form of radical self-care. If you have trouble differentiating your feelings from those of others, tend to absorb other people's feelings, find yourself weighed down or preoccupied by the energy of others, have trouble saying no, or identify as a highly sensitive person, a people pleaser, or empath, the Boundaries Breath is a great tool to have in your self-care kit.

When I was younger, I wore my empathy like a badge of honor. While I do believe that being sensitive is a gift, empathy on the other hand is often a marker of growing up in a dysfunctional household or experiencing relational trauma. This can lead to feeling overly responsible for other people's emotions, not being able to say no, or constantly changing yourself to make other people happy. True empaths, and I have worked with many over the years, take on other people's emotions, thoughts, and even physical symptoms. What happens when you're an empath is that your energy centers are too open and your personal boundaries are weak, perhaps nonexistent, therefore allowing other people's energy to come in. When these two energies mix, it disrupts your own nervous system and makes it difficult to distinguish your feelings from the other person's. In this state of confusion, it's challenging to make decisions with your own best interest at heart.

Oftentimes we absorb other people's energy without realizing it because it's a habit we've had for so long and it works in many subtle ways. The good news is that by taking the time to practice the Boundaries Breath, you will begin to establish strength in your own system so that you have the power to stay in your own lane, differentiate from others, feel less responsible for others, and feel empowered to make saying no part of your life.

Many of the clients I've worked with haven't had luck with the more cognitive psychotherapy interventions around setting boundaries because they didn't address the body. If you feel like you don't have any boundaries and can't sense your body, it's incredibly difficult to try to communicate your needs. What's powerful about the Boundaries Breath is that it works directly with your body through the breath while giving you a visual tool to further support the practice. This combination of breath, visualizing, and eventually vocalizing are key aspects to why the practice is effective.

Boundaries

THE PRACTICE

Take a comfortable seat.

Breathe in and out through the nose for a minute to settle in.

Set your practice intention.

Begin by visualizing a sphere of gold surrounding you on the inhale.

As you exhale, keep that sphere in place, allowing it to settle.

Notice where the edge of the sphere is in relation to your body.

Is it three inches away, one foot, ten?

Make a quick mental note and then come back to your breath.

Keep the sphere in the same place for the next seven minutes as you continue to inhale and exhale.

Take a full minute to release the visual guide of the sphere and settle into yourself.

As you settle, see if any words want to be expressed around your boundary. If so, say them aloud.

Close your practice.

Note any changes you experienced.

Journal.

Be sure to jot down in your notes where the sphere was in relation to your body in your practice session. This is key for boundary work. I suggest practicing daily for two weeks initially to start to establish a new boundary system for your body. After the first two weeks, practice the Boundaries Breath at least three times a week. If you identify as an empath I highly suggest practicing daily for many months to really solidify this practice in your body.

In each practice session after the first, experiment with the distance of the sphere. In some sessions pull it closer to you and in others expand it farther away. Note the changes that come in your journal. After several rounds of practice, you will have a good idea of where the sphere is most comfortable for you. Then work with that distance for at least one week, or more if you choose.

The Boundaries Breath can bring up big emotions, childhood, and family-of-origin work. As uncomfortable as it might be in the moment, it's actually a really good thing. Whatever surfaces during your practice sessions and while you're out in the world is ready to be explored, healed, and integrated.

Learning to set boundaries has been one of the most challenging and rewarding practices of my life, and I am still learning each day. In the beginning, my boundaries were really harsh and intense because I had to break the habit of years and years of putting others' needs before my own and merging with them on a regular basis. Today my boundaries, while firm, are much softer, and actually I enjoy saying no and practicing self-care.

Cleanse

One of the first breathing practices I learned in my early yoga days was *kapalabhati*, or "skull-shining breath." I found this practice difficult and intense but loved how it made me feel afterward. The Cleanse Breath is a modified version of the classic pranayama technique, and though it's less intense on the system, it has similar effects and benefits.

As I mentioned in the section entitled "Breath: The Foundational Tool," the majority of the toxins in our body are released through our exhale. The Cleanse Breath places emphasis on the exhale with a slight drawing in of the abdomen to gently cleanse and tone the respiratory system while purifying and refreshing the body and mind. The Cleanse Breath is also an excellent choice for clearing the mind of cluttered thinking.

Think of the Cleanse Breath as your one-stop practice to release unwanted toxins in the body and uplift the mind. This practice also energizes the nervous system and rejuvenates brain cells by increasing oxygen supply in the body.

Cleanse

THE PRACTICE

Sit in a comfortable position with your spine straight and tall.

Place your hands on your knees, palms facing up.

Set your practice intention.

Breathe in and out through the nose for one minute to settle in.

Place one hand on your abdomen and open your eyes.

Inhale deeply.

As you exhale, gently contract your lower belly, releasing the breath through the nose in a short burst.

As you release your abdomen, breath will flow into your lungs automatically.

Take ten rounds of breath in this manner.

Relax, perhaps with your eyes closed, and notice the sensations in your body.

Complete two more cycles of ten rounds of breath with a relaxing period afterward.

Close your practice.

Journal.

This is one of the most advanced practices in the book. I highly suggest that you develop a breathwork routine for at least two months with other practices first before trying the Cleanse Breath.

If you are pregnant, have just given birth, or are menstruating, you should avoid this practice. In addition, if you are recently recovering from surgery, have high blood pressure, a heart condition, or a respiratory condition, use caution when practicing the Cleanse Breath. Go slowly and trust your body; if it feels like too much, stop.

The traditional practice of *kapalabhati* instructions uses language like "force the exhale out of the nose" and the practice is done very rapidly, which can cause dizziness or lightheadedness. The Cleanse Breath was designed to be a softer and more gentle way to reap the benefits of this classic pranayama practice without placing unnecessary stress on the body or nervous system.

Connection

Lack of connection is a serious issue facing our world today. As we become increasingly dependent on computers and devices to do many of the things that we have done for ourselves in the past, from grocery shopping, to dating, to communicating, we live less in community and more in isolation. While the long-term effects are still in question, research already shows that our health, vitality, and resilience are greatly impacted by our diminishing everyday social connections.

Humans are social creatures. We are by design meant to interact and relate with those around us. As our world continues to make these technological advancements, many of which are very useful and important, it's equally important that we not get lost from our very human need to connect to others in real time and in real life.

Studies have shown for decades that babies cannot survive without contact from other humans and that we as a species cannot thrive in isolation. The remedy for isolation is connection, and the breath is such an incredible invitation to connect with our most fundamental needs and desires. When the Connection Breath is practiced with another person, it is transformative for both people. When our systems sync up with one another, we tap into a group nervous system that is both regulating and healing. The Connection Breath reminds us that taking a few minutes to sit and breathe with another person is a powerful antidote to many of our daily struggles and is a healing balm that supports us in times of uncertainty. We are meant to hold each other, lift each other up, and witness each other. The Connection Breath is one way to do this.

Connection

THE PRACTICE

Find a comfortable seat facing your partner.

Breathe in and out through the nose for a minute to settle in.

Set your practice intentions.

When ready, turn around and sit with your backs touching.

Breathe slowly in and out through your noses.

Without rushing or speaking to each other, allow your breaths to begin to sync up.

Breathe in sync for eight minutes.

Gently release the practice and allow your breath to flow naturally.

Rest for a few moments and notice how you feel; also notice what happens with the breath.

Journal.

Spend a few minutes discussing what came up for each of you.

Close your practice with a hug.

Be gentle with the process of finding your way to the breaths flowing in sync. Sometimes this happens quickly and other times it takes a while. Stay present with the journey of meeting each other where you are and trust that the process is unfolding exactly as it needs to.

This is an excellent practice to do with partners, friends, and children. I suggest this practice if you're feeling isolated, if you're in an argument with your partner or friend, or when two children aren't getting along. This practice is a great connector and a wonderful way to drop into your body and get to the root of what's happening emotionally.

The Connection Breath is also known for bringing up our work around giving and receiving. I've taught this practice for years in groups, and there are always some students who talk about their feelings of inadequacy, judgment, needing to be in charge, or resisting leaning into the other person to find the flow. This is a very powerful practice that needs to be done with care and respect for ourselves and our partners.

Dreaming

Working with your dreams is a very informative way to connect to the subconscious. Certain breathwork practices naturally lend themselves to working with the subconscious. The Dreaming Breath is a gentle practice for the evening that can be a fun way to release residual stress in the mind and body, and direct or engage with your dreams.

I had a boyfriend out of high school whose father had been recording his dreams for over twenty years. I remember being in his home library one winter looking at stacks of notebooks in which he had recorded his dreams first thing every morning. While I didn't start a dream practice then, though I wish I had, that experience stuck with me, and later in grad school I started writing down my dreams and diving more into my own subconscious.

Dreams are often thought of as our minds' burning off the stress of the day, which is why they can often be stressful. When we work through major life transitions, like moving, switching jobs, or ending relationships, our dreams tend to be fast paced and involve running away from something, escaping situations, or any myriad of anxiety-provoking activities. This is a very common experience and one that I have found the Dreaming Breath can help with immensely.

When you practice the Dreaming Breath in bed before you fall asleep, it serves as a gentle way to release the thoughts of a cluttered mind and guide your nervous system into rest-and-digest mode. If you're even a little bit less stressed as you fall asleep, the Dreaming Breath is likely to change your dreams over time.

If you're interested in directing or engaging with your dreams, this practice works wonders as well. Our minds like direction, and when we're in a relaxed state from the breathing, it's easier to direct our minds to specific experiences we want to focus on while we're sleeping. The Dreaming Breath is also useful if you have big questions that you're seeking answers for. You can ask one of them as you drift off to sleep in your practice and look forward to what surfaces at night.

Dreaming

THE PRACTICE

Get in bed, lie down on your back, and make yourself comfortable.

Set your intention.

Begin breathing in and out through your nose slowly for a few rounds.

Next, extend your inhale and exhale, allowing for a natural rhythm to take shape.

Continue extending your inhales and exhales until they are as long as possible without stress or strain on the body or respiratory system.

Repeat the practice until you fall asleep.

Journal first thing in the morning about your dreams.

NOTES

Keep your breathwork journal by your bed so that as soon as you wake up you can roll over and start writing. It's important to get those notes down ASAP because as you start to wake up your dreams begin to fade. If you have difficulty remembering your dreams, you can set an intention before you go to bed as part of the Dreaming Breath to remember your dreams. This can help immensely.

Energy

Let's face it, we all feel tired at times and need an extra pick-me-up. Whether you're kicking that a.m. caffeine habit, dragging the kids off to school, or feeling a midday lull coming on, the Energy Breath is a fun way to engage your breath and body for an anytime uplifting boost.

In just one minute, the Energy Breath oxygenates your brain and blood, giving you the natural fuel you need to keep going. This is a favorite of my clients because it's unexpected and usually makes them laugh. I use the Energy Breath a great deal with my corporate clients as well because it's fun to practice in groups and gets everyone ready to head back to work with clarity, vibrancy, and focus.

The Energy Breath can be practiced first thing in the morning or throughout the day when you notice your energy dwindling.

Energy

THE PRACTICE

Take your position.

Set your practice intention.

Sit or stand tall, lengthening the spine.

Rest your arms at your sides.

Inhale through your nose and lift your arms up to the sky.

Exhale.

Inhale deeply; as you exhale, bend your elbows and pull your arms down so that your hands are aligned with your head.

Inhale and raise your arms back up, exhale and bring them down.

Repeat this practice for one full minute.

When finished, release your arms all the way down and rest for another minute.

Close your practice.

Journal.

NOTES

If you're at work and notice other coworkers are tired, you might suggest a one-minute Energy Breath break to revive your capacity to focus. This is also a wonderful practice to do with children if they have too much energy; you can have them slow this practice down as a way to help them ground and focus.

Focus

The Focus Breath is one of the first practices I developed for clients who showed up to their sessions in need of mental, emotional, and energetic reorganizing. Whether they wanted to rein in their scattered energy from sitting in traffic on their way to our session, had a recent conversation on repeat in their mind, or felt bogged down from their day, the Focus Breath cut through the muck, reorienting them to the present moment.

The majority of the breathing techniques in this book are to be practiced in and out through the nose. The Clearing, Focus, and Intuition Breath practices are different, as they require an open-mouthed exhale. Exhaling through the mouth is a very effective way to move energy out of the body. This type of exhale allows for a faster and fuller release of breath, and is an active way to shift your energy.

The Focus Breath invites the use of a specific sound, or mantra, on the exhale. Sound in the form of mantra has been used for centuries in Eastern cultures as a technique for quieting the mind. New research on the brain and behavior has shown that these mantras are very effective for changing the state of the brain. In Sanskrit, *mantra* translates as "tool or instrument of the mind." Mantras are made up of short words meant to be repeated. Traditionally, mantras are practiced silently or aloud through the exhale.

I've studied various short and long forms of Sanskrit mantras for years. I discovered that the silent mantra practice worked great on the mental plane, but it didn't help me drop into my body. After years of experimenting, it became clear that vocalizing the mantra on the exhale is the more effective way to relieve the mind from scattered thinking. I work with the HA-AA-AA mantra because it is easy to say and has no literal meaning. When spoken aloud, this sound carries a vibration that keeps you out of the mind and leads you deeper into the breath.

Focus

THE PRACTICE

Find a comfortable position with both feet on the floor.

Breathe in and out through the nose for a minute to settle in.

Set your practice intention.

Inhale through the nose for two counts.

Exhale through the mouth, sounding out the word HA-AA-AA in your regular speaking tone for as long as you can without force or strenuous effort.

Repeat inhaling through the nose and exhaling HA-AA-AA for three minutes.

Next, spend a full minute breathing in and out through the nose.

Close your practice.

Journal.

NOTES

Have fun with this practice. There aren't many spaces where it's appropriate to just make noise like this, so enjoy the process of letting it out and clearing your mind. Sometimes my clients like to make the HA-AA-AA very loud; this can be great for a couple of rounds if you find that your mind is having trouble getting on board.

The Focus Breath is useful to practice at the end of a long day or when you find yourself in a chaotic or stressful moment. It's also a client favorite as a traffic remedy.

Forgiveness

The Forgiveness Breath practice is like graduate school for emotional and relational intelligence. It's a slightly more evolved cousin to the Gratitude Breath (page 75) and is a key building block in our personal and spiritual development.

I remember hearing in Al-Anon years ago that resentments are like drinking poison and expecting the other person to get sick. Intense? Yes. Uncomfortably true? Also yes. When we're angry or resentful at someone, ourselves included, it compromises our health and our ability to make clear decisions. When you feel resentful, your body is in a state of stress, and hormones such as cortisol and adrenaline are flowing through your bloodstream diluting endorphins and other feel-good chemicals. Prolonged stress, in this case resentment, has detrimental effects on our health because our bodies are not designed to function with those stress hormones at such high levels for long periods of time.

Without dealing with our feelings of resentment, they grow and fester at an alarming rate. This is in part because the hormones that ramp up our system also increase heart rate, slow down digestion, and weaken immune function. Making a conscious effort to get to the bottom of our resentment and shift our subconscious beliefs is a radical and necessary practice for the health of our hearts, minds, bodies, and communities.

Forgiveness is also about taking healthy responsibility. Oftentimes when we do the work of unpacking our resentments, we can flip in the other direction and be incredibly hard on ourselves, willing to take on way too much responsibility for ourselves and others. When we start to practice the Forgiveness Breath, it helps us keep the focus on our own actions and hearts in a way that is reasonable. The Forgiveness Breath is a healing salve that helps us tune into our own vulnerability, hold witness space for ourselves, and allow ourselves to be perfectly imperfect.

Forgiveness

THE PRACTICE

Find a comfortable position lying down.

Set your intention.

Breathe in and out through the nose for a minute to settle in.

When ready, take a long, gentle breath in through the nose.

On your exhale, say one thing out loud that you forgive yourself for.

Repeat this practice for several minutes until you feel finished.

Rest for a minute.

Close your practice.

Journal.

NOTES

This is a nourishing self-care practice to do at the end of the day, especially on those days where you feel like you made more mistakes than you care to admit. It's also a very healing practice to do when you find yourself focusing on others.

When using this practice to forgive others, say what you forgive them for on the exhale. I've found it most effective to focus on one person at a time. This keeps your energy clear and directional during practice and allows for deeper insight into the root of the particular resentment.

Gratitude

Gratitude has been steadily gaining popularity in the psychology and wellness fields for years. With leaders like Oprah, Brené Brown, and Elizabeth Gilbert singing its praises, it's no wonder this powerful and magical practice has officially become mainstream.

Gratitude in its most essential form is the quality of being thankful and a willingness to express appreciation. I first learned about gratitude from my twelve-step sponsor and started a practice around it while in rehab. At the time I struggled to come up with anything that I was grateful for. I was twenty-one, I believed my life was over, and I felt that I was a disappointment to myself and my family. With encouragement from my sponsor, I began writing very short lists each evening before bed of what I was grateful for that day. It started with entries like, I am alive, I can breathe, and I can walk. It later developed into lists so long my hand would get tired from writing. This practice fundamentally changed my life, and it's the reason I created the Gratitude Breath.

We enter this world on an inhale and we leave it on an exhale. Every breath between those two is a gift. The Gratitude Breath is very close to my heart and reminds me each time I practice how far I've come, how determined my spirit is, and how deep my desire is to hold space for others to follow their own breath.

Gratitude

THE PRACTICE

Find a comfortable position lying down.

Set your intention.

Breathe in and out through the nose for a minute to settle in.

When ready, take a long, gentle breath through the nose.

On your exhale, say one thing out loud that you are grateful for.

Repeat this practice for several minutes until you have
exhausted your list.

Rest for a minute.

Close your practice.

Journal.

NOTES

This practice is wonderful at night before bed. It's a relaxing and affirming way to fall asleep, especially when the day has been riddled with challenges and you have a glass-half-empty outlook.

You can also practice the Gratitude Breath anytime you feel like you are caught in a negative mental loop; this practice is excellent to do in conjunction with the Negative Thinking Breath (page 103). Do a few rounds of the Negative Thinking Breath and follow that up with a few cycles of the Gratitude Breath.

Grief

Loss is part of life, and the deep sorrow and grief we experience can create a feeling of stagnation and the inability to move freely. Because the weight of grief can feel so heavy, even a little breathwork and shift in body posture can bring relief.

Changing our breath and position as a way to open the stagnation and inactivity in the body can do wonders for the dense emotions that often accompany grief. The heaviness that comes with grief can make you want to curl up into a ball, slump down, and protect your heart. When clients come to sessions grieving, they often present a very shallow or breath holding pattern that they aren't always aware of. Sometimes they report that they feel they are gasping for air as if they are stuck under water and don't have the energy to come up for air until the last second. All of these physical manifestations of grief impact our ability to process our feelings.

If we aren't inhaling enough oxygen and failing to exhale enough carbon dioxide, this can add to the fatigue and mental fog that comes with grief and can intensify many of the normal grief reactions that we go through as part of our process. Taking long, slow inhales and exhales into the abdomen is the ideal way to support the grief process. Whether you have a tendency to wallow, keep yourself too busy to feel, or do some combination of the two, the Grief Breath practice creates the space for you to touch into your emotions in a safe and contained way.

In the Grief Breath, I've combined this slow, deep breath with one of my favorite yoga poses that is very restorative to an overworked nervous system. The legs-up-the-wall pose puts the diaphragm in a position where it is easier to exhale. With gravity to support the exhale, the inhale naturally begins to deepen and lengthen on its own. Connecting this pose to breathwork also slows down the heart rate, which sends a message to the brain that all is well in the body, thus allowing us to relax more deeply. As we begin to self-regulate, we strengthen our capacity to feel what needs to be felt in whatever stage of grief we are in.

Grief

THE PRACTICE

Sit on a mat or blanket close to the wall.

Carefully roll onto your side and extend your legs up the wall.

Adjust yourself so that your bottom and the backs of your legs are connected to the wall and your torso is aligned with your hips.

Rest your arms by your sides.

Set your practice intention.

Recheck your positioning to make sure that you feel aligned.

Begin breathing gently and slowly in and out through the nose for eight minutes.

Notice any changes in your breath without trying to adjust it in any way.

Allow your body to feel supported by the wall and floor, continuing to sink and relax with each exhale.

If distressing thoughts or images come to mind, gently return your attention to your breath.

At the end of the eight minutes, rest and observe how you feel.

When you're ready to come out of the posture, bend your knees into your chest and roll to one side.

Place your hands on the floor and push yourself up.

Close your practice.

Journal.

NOTES

If you find yourself wanting to practice longer than eight minutes, please feel free. You can do this practice up to twenty minutes once you get comfortable and familiar with it. If you are a practicing yogi, you are welcome to use a bolster under your hips for a soft heart opening that will add another layer to the Grief Breath.

Please note, if you are more than three months pregnant or have neck issues, a detached retina, glaucoma, or high blood pressure, do not practice with your legs up the wall. An alternative to this pose is to practice the breathwork portion in a seated position that is very comfortable, keeping your hips and legs at the same height if possible. Propping yourself up on a couch or bed with pillows behind your back and under your knees is a great way to allow your body to relax so that you can access your breath and eventually touch into the grief.

Grounding

The Grounding Breath has become a practice that I teach all of my clients at the beginning of our time together. It's foundational. We cannot heal and thrive if we cannot first inhabit our bodies. I have a history of sexual violence and trauma, and this Grounding Breath has been an essential piece of my healing journey. Those experiences, like many traumas so many of us experience, took me far out of my body. The Grounding Breath was the tool that I created to bring me back to my body and to gain confidence in my body. That helped me worry less about the future, feel less sad about the past, and open up to the reality of the here and now.

Over time, accessing my Grounding Breath has enabled me to stay present through many of the most joyous and challenging moments of my life. There are still times when I check out of my body, and they are mostly with my partner when we're navigating difficult experiences. The beauty today is that I am aware that I am checking out and have the Grounding Breath as the anchor to bring me back into the experience of the present moment.

The Grounding Breath is a potent practice for dropping into your body, connecting to the earth, and encouraging your system to self-regulate. It's also a great practice if you get frequent headaches.

Grounding

THE PRACTICE

Take a moment to settle into your chair with your feet flat on the floor.

Set your practice intention.

Inhale and exhale gently through your nose for five cycles.

Next, bring your awareness to the soles of your feet.

With a slow inhale, imagine drawing up energy from the earth into the soles of your feet, up to your knees and back toward your hips.

On the exhale, imagine the energy flowing from your hips to your knees, and then back down through the soles of your feet to the earth.

Continue to sync the energy revolutions with your breath for five minutes.

Let go of the revolutions and allow your breath to settle into a passive state.

Sit for one more minute.

Close your practice.

Journal.

NOTES

Take your time with this practice; there is no need to rush. Begin with five minutes and work your way up to ten. If you're new to breathwork and it feels scary, that is okay. Start with just a minute or two.

If you feel your temperature rise or the sensation of feeling heavier in your body, this is normal and is a sign that you are becoming more grounded.

This is a great practice to do in the morning to start your day. It can be done alone or as the beginning to a longer practice session, which is how I often recommend it to clients after they have practiced it by itself for a couple of weeks. No need to practice longer than ten minutes. The Grounding Breath can also be done at your desk at work for a needed break to plug in to yourself, or at the end of the day as a way to reset and transition to the evening.

Intimacy

One of the most intimate acts of connection we can practice is breathing with our partners. When we show up fully and sit with each other in our realness, we create a container of safety and love, which allows us to become vulnerable.

Over the years, I have had the honor of working with many couples in my practice. What I often see at the beginning is a lack of connection around intimacy. They might be exceptional communicators, highly successful in business, great friends, amazing parents, or brilliant creatives, but something feels off to them in their connection.

I created the Intimacy Breath as a first step to support these couples in building connection with each other. Intimacy is a by-product of vulnerability, and vulnerability is the foundation for safe, loving, and meaningful relationships. By setting the content of their relationships aside and using the breath as their guide, I have seen couples reignite their passion, joy, and tenderness for each other in just a few practice sessions.

As I discuss in the section entitled "Breath: The Foundational Tool," our breath is inextricably linked to our emotions. When couples practice the Intimacy Breath, often what surfaces is a series of revelations about the behaviors, beliefs, and family-of-origin experiences that are impacting their present relationship. These awakenings lead them to deeper inquiry about their personal growth, allowing them to see the next steps they need to take as individuals and as couples to cultivate the connection they are seeking.

The Intimacy Breath is an updated version of an ancient eye-gazing practice I learned years ago in a yoga teacher training. I took the eye-gazing practice and added touch and synchronized breath to bring this practice out of the mental realm and drop it fully into the body. Nonsexual touch is a key component of building intimacy and is a potent spiritual tool for holding witness space for each other. Often the couples I see are so caught up in their stories and worries that they don't spend much time together fully embodied. The Intimacy Breath is a gentle yet powerful way for couples to come into connection with each other.

Intimacy

THE PRACTICE

Find a comfortable seat facing your partner.

Breathe in and out through the nose for a minute to settle in.

Set your practice intentions.

To begin, take your left hand and place it on your partner's heart, resting your right hand on your thigh, palm facing up.

Have your partner copy you.

Adjust your positions as needed.

Continue breathing in and out through your noses.

Keep your eyes open and gaze into each other's left eyes while breathing.

Slowly, without talking, begin to synchronize your breath.

Do not rush this process. Let it evolve naturally.

Continue breathing together, gazing, and holding your hands on each other's hearts for five minutes.

Release your left hands and allow your breath to flow naturally.

Rest for a few moments, continuing with your gaze.

Journal.

Spend a few minutes discussing what came up for each of you.

Close your practice with a hug.

If your left arm gets tired during the practice, let it rest with your palm facing up on your left thigh. If you can only hold your left arm up for a couple of minutes, that is great! Over time it will become stronger and be able to hold that position for longer. Getting a few minutes of touch in the beginning of the practice is how you get your bodies to tune into each other quickly, and this allows for the breath to synchronize effectively.

Practicing the Intimacy Breath often brings up emotions that are stored in the body, and the practice can feel quite vulnerable. You might experience a range of emotions and that is okay. It's not unheard of to let out tears or laughter during this practice. It's also normal to feel scattered as you begin to regulate with your partner and slow things down.

I suggest practicing the Intimacy Breath three to four times each week for two months and then one to two times after that to stay connected. My clients enjoy this practice after a long day at work as a way to sync up with each other before starting their evenings, on mornings when they can stay in bed a little longer, before a difficult conversation, when they are navigating tough experiences, or anytime they feel their relationship needs a little connection boost.

Intuition

Getting in tune with our life force via the breath is a powerful way to tap into our inner wisdom. Intuition comes through the strongest and is most accurate when we are embodied. It's hard to access your gut feelings when you're someplace other than your body. The key with the Intuition Breath is to develop a baseline of presence so that when you're out in the world it's easier to stay grounded, clear, and open to receiving whatever information wants to be shared with you.

Intuition gives us the ability to know something without analytical reasoning. It is often described as a feeling, a sixth sense, or that subtle knowing that you can't quite put your finger on. The intuitive channel is a potent source of creativity and information. Cultivating a relationship with your intuition offers you an invaluable guidance system that supports you in all areas of your life.

Everyone has the potential to be intuitive. It's part of our biological makeup. While many people are quick to dismiss their intuition because it can seem irrational, this leads to an undeveloped intuition and cuts off access to a very important function of our brain. Intuitive information can seem illogical because intuition operates from our right brain and by other parts of our brain that have been around since prehistoric times, known as the *limbic* and *reptilian* systems. Our slower, more analytical left brain, home to the neocortex, is where people spend most of their time, which is why it can feel foreign to trust the quick instincts that are associated with intuition.

Most breathwork practices can support intuition development if they are grounded in being in your body. With practice and presence you can develop your intuitive skills, which can serve as a creative and practical way to learn about yourself, make decisions, and dive deeper into your creativity and self-expression. The Intuitive Breath is slow and steady like many practices in this book, as it's meant to ultimately follow the inherent wisdom of your body, which is the key piece in honing your intuitive abilities. Intuitive hits can come through in sounds, images, and physical sensations. In order to have access to this information we have to be in our instinctual right brain, not meandering around on the left side.

Intuition

THE PRACTICE

Get into a comfortable position lying down.

Set your practice intention.

Begin breathing in and out through your nose for a minute to settle in.

When you're ready, inhale slowly through your mouth.

Exhale gently through your mouth.

Take your time to find a steady flow and cycle with each round of breath.

Repeat in this way for at least ten minutes.

When you're ready to finish, breathe in and out through your nose for couple of minutes to integrate the work.

Close your practice.

Journal.

NOTES

The Intuitive Breath is the only practice in this book that uses an open-mouth inhale and exhale. This style of breathing is very opening for the energetic body, putting us in contact with our inner wisdom. It can feel strange in the beginning, and you might feel a little lightheaded. If you do, slow the breath down more; if that doesn't help, switch to breathing in and out through your nose for a little while and then go back to open-mouth breathing when you feel ready.

I suggest practicing the Intuitive Breath for at least ten minutes to receive the benefits. It can take a few minutes for your body to get used to it and find your steady rhythm. You want to have as much time in the flow of the practice as possible. When you are more familiar with it, you're welcome to breathe for longer, up to twenty-five minutes.

The key with intuition is to trust what comes up and not try too hard to figure it out. If learning to use your intuition as a guide for your life is a new practice, I encourage you to experiment and have fun. Be sure to take notes on what information comes through during your breath sessions and, if you want to take it a step further, throughout your day as well.

The Intuitive Breath is designed to help you access your inner wisdom on and off the mat, so to speak. The goal is to build your intuitive muscle so that you have a deeper connection to yourself, your purpose, and the guiding forces that are here to support you along the way.

Joy

Stress is becoming a public health crisis. Millennials are currently the most stressed-out generation according to the American Psychological Association's 2017 Stress in America snapshot. This rise in stress is accompanied by stress-related symptoms and poor health and wellness. Over the years, I've found that a good remedy to help our bodies and minds manage the increasing demands on our day-to-day lives is the practice of joy.

It can sound strange to cultivate joy in a culture where more than half of Americans report being unhappy in some aspect of their lives. Focusing on happiness is futile because it's a fleeting emotion that is often based on something outside of ourselves. Joy, on the other hand, doesn't depend on outside circumstances or events. Joy is an attitude of the heart and is found within each of us if we are willing to show up and cultivate it.

When I began my breathwork practice, I recognized I needed to shift my relationship to stress. I began connecting to my authentic self through slowing down in my work life (it's very difficult to get down that deep when you're super busy). I felt less need to chase momentary happiness through outside experiences or validation. I was organically drawn to desire joy and see if it was possible to make it a more regular state of being. I wondered if it was possible to cultivate joy from the inside out.

This personal inquiry led me to develop the Joy Breath practice as a way to train myself to be more joyful. I took my cues from the Laughter Yoga community and created a playful practice that can be done anytime you need a mood shift or want to spend time practicing joy on your own.

In addition to breathing, I use laughter in the Joy Breath because it's an excellent way to create good sensations in the body, which in turn create positive thoughts in the mind. An interesting scientific fact is that the body cannot differentiate between fake and real laughter. You get the same endorphin release and positive neurotransmitters that stimulate our brains, nervous systems, and immune systems no matter why you are laughing or how you started.

I've used several variations of the Joy Breath with clients who at first are hesitant because it's a little strange. Afterward they end up really liking the practice and are often surprised by how much space it opens up for joy in other areas of their life. At its core the Joy Breath is about being present, and as we become more present it is easier to access joy and experience it for longer stretches of time.

Joy

THE PRACTICE

Stand up tall with your feet hip distance apart.

Put a slight bend in your knees and let your arms rest at your sides.

Set your practice intention.

Take a few cycles of breath through the nose to settle in.

Next, inhale deeply while raising your arms up toward the sky.

Hold your breath for a couple of seconds.

Release your arms down by your sides as you laugh out loud.

Repeat this ten times, being sure to breathe and laugh as deeply as possible.

Rest for a few moments and notice how you feel.

Close your practice.

Journal.

NOTES

The Joy Breath is an invitation to switch your body and brain chemistry, thus changing the way you feel from the inside out. This is a great practice to do anytime you want to shift your state, uplift yourself, and take care of yourself in a fun and unconventional way.

Though it might feel awkward at first, the Joy Breath is excellent to practice with friends, family members, and kids. With just a few seconds of deep belly laughs, you experience just how contagious joy really is and how easy it is to cultivate with intention and willingness.

This practice is meant to serve as an entryway to connecting with joy. Feel free to lengthen the time of your practice as you see fit or add some organic, gentle movements into it. You really can't go wrong if you follow the flow of your body, breath, and of course laughter.

Letting Go

One of the biggest questions I hear with new clients is, How can I let go? Instinctually, they know they are hanging on to too much and are at a loss for how to release the energetic buildup. As you've been learning, freely moving breath in the body is a key sign of health and wellness and a marker of our energetic vitality and strength. So often it's the beliefs that don't serve us, the damaging stories that we tell over and over (reinforcing those beliefs), and our behavior patterns (created as a result of those beliefs) that are the root cause of many of our emotional, mental, and physical issues.

One of my favorite sayings from Al-Anon is *let go or be dragged.* The reality is that most of us aren't willing to let go until we absolutely have to. We understand that we need to drop our baggage and live lighter, but just how do we do that? The concept of letting go is elusive at best and is tossed around so freely in the wellness community without any tangible way of practicing. The Letting Go Breath was created as an antidote to all the spiritual jargon around letting go. It's a practice that you can do no matter where you are on the letting-go spectrum.

The Letting Go Breath is a way to receive support from your life force so that you have more freedom and spaciousness in your body, heart, and mind. When we're able to let go with our breath and bodies, it breaks down the constructs in our minds that keep us bound to beliefs that are restrictive and draining. While I would love to report that I haven't been dragged since hearing those words over a decade ago, the truth is I have, but it happens much less frequently and my belief system has been slowly reorganizing itself and evolving with practice and patience.

Letting Go

THE PRACTICE

Stand up tall with your feet hip distance apart.

Put a slight bend in your knees and let your arms rest at your sides.

Set your practice intention.

Take a few cycles of breath through the nose to settle in.

Inhale deeply while raising your arms up toward the sky.

Hinge at your hips and release your arms down to the ground, bending your knees as you exhale a giant sigh through your open mouth.

Repeat this ten times, being sure to inhale and sigh as deeply as possible.

Rest for a few moments and notice how you feel.

Close your practice.

Journal.

NOTES

This combination of movement and breath is a wonderful way to bring your body on board for the practice of letting go. Being able to sync your breath with the movement of this practice brings your heart and mind into alignment while giving you the spaciousness to release what is no longer necessary.

Letting go is a process, and it takes time. When you set your practice intention, keep it simple and in current time. Don't expect a belief that was established in childhood to suddenly be gone after ten breaths. It's important to be realistic about this practice and also stick with issues that you are facing in the current moment, perhaps how a particular belief is manifesting in the present.

The Letting Go Breath is my go-to practice between clients to shift my energy, release anything that might be lingering from the session, and reorient me to the present moment. It's also a wonderful practice to do at the end of the day to leave the day's activities and events behind you. Think of the Letting Go Breath as an opportunity to have a clean slate and a fresh start.

Negative Thinking

The old adage goes, you can't fix a problem using the thing that caused it in the first place. Never has this truism applied more than it does to negative thinking. If the mind is on a negative thought spiral, then the mind is not the most effective tool to shift that thought pattern; the breath is.

This breathwork practice was developed for anyone who is caught in a mental loop, and let's face it: most of the loops we get stuck in aren't very positive. Have you ever noticed how easy it is to focus on what isn't going right or well? Most of us, if given twenty compliments and one criticism, spend most of our energy concentrating on the latter. This isn't because there is something wrong with us or that we haven't done enough work on ourselves. This attention to negativity is part of our brain's hardware; it's one of the reasons humans have survived as long as we have. However, this hardware is in need of an upgrade, and the breath can help us get there.

As we're learning from current research, changing our breath patterns is a very effective way to change our mental and emotional states. The Negative Thinking practice is a way to break the negative cycle. Over time, this can become a key tool in your self-care kit, putting that giant computer inside your head to better use.

Negative Thinking

THE PRACTICE

Set your practice intention.

Take three small consecutive breaths through your nose.

Exhale through the mouth in the same manner.

Repeat this for two minutes.

Take a full minute to rest and observe any changes.

Close your practice.

Journal.

NOTES

If you feel lightheaded during this practice, try it seated until you are more accustomed to taking in more oxygen, or exhale through the nose instead of the mouth.

Breathing through the mouth in this practice helps to clear energy more quickly than an exhale through the nose. This can be a faster way to change our state and, in the case of a negative thought loop, can be very supportive for making that change happen quickly.

If you're still struggling with the negative thought loop afterward (and don't worry if you are; sometimes those loops have a seriously strong hold, especially if they stem from childhood), this practice is great to do in tandem with the Gratitude Breath (page 75). Begin with the Negative Thinking Breath and then flow into the Gratitude Breath. This is a potent combination for shifting the pattern and finding relief.

Open Heart

Physiologically, our hearts pump blood through our circulatory system. Energetically, the heart is considered the seat of compassion, love, and wisdom. Research from the Heart Math Institute has now shown that cultivating a heart-focused practice—directing your attention to your heart—can significantly influence your awareness, creativity, emotional intelligence, and ability to self-regulate.

When our heart is open energetically, it is easy to connect to people, have a deep, compassionate knowing, and freely access our innate wisdom. When our heart is closed, we usually feel cut off from others, sad, withdrawn, and have a difficult time hearing our intuitive voice.

The Open Heart Breath is an invitation to take a moment to access what is happening in your heart and set aside time to invite in love and softness. This practice is very subtle because it invites you to listen to your heart in a new way. In order to hear what your heart has to say, your nervous system needs to be settled. This will give you direct access to your heart's wisdom.

In my practice with clients, one of the biggest issues I see is people giving too much and not receiving enough. The Open Heart practice is an offering that you give yourself when you want to call in more love, joy, compassion, intuitive knowing, and self-care. It works wonders to soothe sad or painful emotions while also supporting connection and receptivity.

The Open Heart Breath is a powerful practice to commit to when you're going through challenges in relationships and a beautiful practice to teach children, as this breathwork will support their innate curious and intuitive nature. This practice also helps you cultivate self-worth.

Open Heart

THE PRACTICE

First, gather any supports like a blanket or pillow that will make your practice feel cozy.

Lie down in a position that makes you feel very comfortable.

Set your practice intention.

Place your hands over your heart in a way that brings the most ease in your body and gently close your eyes.

Take a long, deep breath in through your nose.

Exhale through your nose one to two counts longer than your inhale.

Repeat for a few cycles until you begin to settle.

When you feel settled, bring your awareness to your heart.

Ask this question to yourself or aloud, "Dear Heart, is there something you have been trying to tell me?"

Continue to breathe and wait for a response.

If after a while nothing comes, ask again and wait.

When your heart has finished, say to it silently or aloud, "Thank you. I am here for you. I love you."

Repeat this two more times.

Release your hands to your sides and let the awareness of your breath go. Rest for a few minutes.

Close your practice.

Journal.

Go slowly with this practice. If your heart doesn't have anything to say to you after you ask twice, do not be discouraged. Sometimes it can take a while for it to open up. Stay committed to connecting with your heart and over time it will soften. It is important to listen to your heart without judgment. Often our hearts speak quietly because our minds are full of judgments and fears about what they are saying. An essential aspect to an open heart is giving your heart the space to communicate freely. This can be a very emotional practice, so if feelings surface, allow them to rise and fall like your breath.

If you're going through a big life challenge that is connected to loss or major transition, big emotions might surface. Give yourself space and time to move through those feelings. Trust your process and talk to your heart; it has so much love and wisdom to share with you.

Pain Relief

A simple breathwork practice can have incredible effects on physical pain. One of our natural reflexes is to hold our breath when in or anticipating pain. This impulse ends up causing more discomfort in the body, as it creates stagnation and contraction. When the air is able to flow more freely in the body, pain reduces significantly.

You might have heard the phrase "breathe into the discomfort." The reason this works is because a very effective way to manage physical pain is to breathe through the experience. For the Pain Relief Breath I instruct to focus the breath into the edges of the discomfort or pain rather than right into the center of it. Working with the edges is a safer and more sustainable way to bring relief. Over time and with practice, the pain center will decrease and more ease will be felt in the area of discomfort. The Pain Relief Breath is also an invitation to notice when we are holding our breath and to begin breathing again (into the discomfort), in a slow and mindful way.

Staying present with uncomfortable and painful sensations as they come up is another way to access relief. This sounds scary but really works. In cases of severe physical trauma and pain, many people will disassociate, a function of the body designed to keep us alive. The Pain Relief Breath helps us stay present through intensely uncomfortable experiences and is a way that we can mindfully explore physical pain.

Pain Relief

THE PRACTICE

Situate yourself in the most comfortable position.

Set your practice intention.

Take long, slow breaths in and out through the nose.

Place a gentle awareness on your area of discomfort or pain.

Breathe slowly around the edges.

Pay attention to whether you hold your breath and return
to breathing.

Practice as long as needed.

Notice any differences.

Close your practice.

Journal.

NOTES

The Pain Relief Breath is a portable practice that is designed for wherever and whenever you need it. I use this practice a great deal while in the dentist's chair (one of my least favorite places to be). I experience a lot of sensitivity and find this practice helps me stay present, calm, and in significantly less discomfort.

It's important when practicing to let go of expectations and attachments to the outcome. This creates unnecessary tension in the mind and body and isn't in service to your practice. I understand that is easier said than done and that physical pain, especially if it's chronic, can have a host of psychological and emotional aspects to it as well. What is most beneficial when practicing the Pain Relief Breath is to do so with an open mind.

As you practice breathing into the pain, trust your body. If your inclination is to take small breaths, do that. Don't force your breath or override it with your mind to try to get relief faster. Even a small amount of breath flow into the area can change the tension pattern in the body, and over time this release will grow.

This practice is also very useful in childbirth, in injury recovery, and for back pain.

Parent and Baby

When babies are born, they are unable to regulate themselves. Over time they learn to self-regulate and develop the skills to self-soothe internally and externally through the infant-caregiver relationship. Babies and children in their early years are dependent on their parents to manage their impulses, emotions, and needs because they do not have the capacity to do it for themselves.

One of the most important jobs of parenting during a child's early years is the responsibility of learning how to self-regulate so that you are modeling that for your little one. As I've discussed throughout this book, the breath is an excellent tool for self-regulation, and it's a wonderful way to connect with your baby.

I've had the privilege of working with many new parents in my practice, and I love it when they bring their little ones to sessions. In each session, I am in awe of the magic that transpires when the parent settles onto the table and begins their breathwork; at some point their little one is ready to join, and sessions typically end with the two of them breathing together in very peaceful, regulated states.

The Parent and Baby Breath is a practice that you can do at any time. It works very well when babies are tired or upset. What has been reported back to me by my clients is that this simple practice is about so much more than the breath (it usually is!). Over time it expands into bonding moments that deepen connection and affirm that no matter what happens in a day, there is always an anchor to bring them back to the moment and to each other.

Parent and Baby

THE PRACTICE

Find a comfortable position.

Set a quick intention.

Begin breathing, slowly and gently, in and out through the nose.

Allow the breath to move in and out of your body in whatever way feels the most nourishing and supportive in the moment.

As you breathe, notice what is happening for your baby and remember that you are regulating your baby.

Continue for a few minutes until you are ready to stop.

Thank your baby for practicing with you.

Close your practice.

Journal if you have the energy and time.

NOTES

I purposefully added a note about journaling because, let's face it, as a parent of an infant you have plenty to do! The main thing is to simply notice what's happening and practice each day.

My clients have found this breathwork practice is a great way to lead into a nap or bedtime as well as breast-feeding. It works just as well for the parents as it does for their children.

Parent and Child Relaxation

Showing our children what healthy relaxation looks like and making it a fun activity can be a great way to connect and give them a lifelong tool for self-care. Each child is different and has a unique set of needs that support them to feel confident, successful, and in control of themselves. The Parent and Child Relaxation Breath is an encouraging practice to help reinforce their personal development and give them space to continue learning to self-regulate.

I often hear from parents that they are looking for meaningful ways to connect with their children, and breathwork is one option. Because it requires a level of presence to practice, the Parent and Child Relaxation Breath can become an activity that everyone looks forward to because it's a time when everyone is fully there.

Years ago while I was on a meditation retreat with Thich Nhat Hanh, he said that the greatest gift we can give our children is our true presence. I heard this over a decade ago and never forgot it. It is something I share with all the parents in my practice, and it always resonates with them in a profound way. A big part of what we're all looking for in that search for meaningful connections with our children and loved ones is the capacity and desire to be fully alive and present in as many moments as possible.

Parent and Child Relaxation

THE PRACTICE

Sit comfortably.

Set an intention together.

Ask your child to start paying attention to their breathing and see what they notice.

Have them place one hand on their belly and you do the same.

Invite them to breathe in through their nose with a closed mouth until they feel their chest expand.

Ask them to hold their breath for one second at the top of the inhale.

Next, invite them to blow the air out through their mouth, as slowly as possible.

Repeat this practice with them until they feel relaxed.

Check in with your child afterward and give them space to talk about what they experienced.

Close the practice together.

Journal if you have the time.

I suggest starting this practice with your child or children around three years old. The inquiry in the beginning of the practice starts getting children to connect to their bodies and their breath and to feel how they are related. It's great to practice sitting up and can also be very effective before a nap or at bedtime to help your child settle.

This breath practice is a wonderful activity for the entire family. It can be a fun ritual to end the week, used before the stress of a big test or homework assignment, or used anytime someone in the family needs a reboot.

Children like things to be colorful, imaginative, and fun. Have them participate in picking out special blankets or toys to bring to the area where you will be practicing. It can also be nice to have soft instrumental music playing in the background. I know several parents whose children love to create a fort-like area for their breathing practice. The key is to get them involved and engaged in the entire process.

The Parent and Child Relaxation Breath is especially useful if your child has trouble self-regulating, is very sensitive, or has a tendency to feel overwhelmed. It can be very difficult for a child to be calm if they don't have an experience of what that feels like. It is important that they practice this several times a week to build the resource into their nervous system. This also increases their ability to integrate the work and have it as a tool they can draw on for the rest of their lives.

Resilience

The ability to bounce back to life, returning stronger than before, is a vital component to our health and well-being. Rather than being overcome by perceived failures, missed opportunities, or issues beyond our control, people who are resilient are able to find a way to carry on and thrive. Resilience is a buzzword in psychology today, and given the enormous amount of stress and pressure people are under, it makes sense. Resilience is just as important today as it was in our cave-dwelling days, and it's important to cultivate this quality in our ever-changing and fast-paced landscape.

Some of the key factors that attribute to resilience are being able to self-regulate, the ability to be flexible while still having healthy boundaries, having a positive outlook, supportive communication skills, and the ability to see failure as an opportunity to grow. Individually, all of these qualities have a great deal of merit on their own. When combined, they make up a person who is able to adapt to their surroundings, accept change, keep things in perspective, and take good care of themselves.

Resilience is made up of actions, behaviors, and beliefs that can be developed by anyone. Cultivating resilience is an individual journey, as we're not all going to respond to situations in the same way. Being resilient doesn't mean that you never feel discomfort or experience distress or heartbreaking life events. In fact, often the road to resilience is paved with adversity, trauma, and a great deal of emotional dysregulation.

The Resilience Breath in many ways could be any breathwork practice that draws you into your center, anchors you in the present, helps you feel alive, and reminds you that you've got this. I have yet to meet anyone who, after a few months of a dedicated breathwork practice, didn't develop greater self-worth, the capacity to be more gentle with themselves, the ability to better regulate the ups and downs of their emotional landscape, and ultimately the awareness to become more embodied.

For many of us, myself included, the journey toward resilience is long, twisty, and riddled with deep sorrow and unexplainable joy. As you come to develop and eventually strengthen your connection to your breath, your inner wisdom, and your life force energy, you will find it easier to maintain flexibility in your life, hang out in the elusive gray areas, relish opportunities for self-discovery, keep things in perspective, be able to heal what needs to be healed, and expand into the person you were meant to be all along.

Resilience

THE PRACTICE

Stand up tall with your feet hip distance apart.

Put a slight bend in your knees and let your arms rest at your sides.

Set your practice intention.

Breathe in and out through your nose for a few cycles to settle in.

Take a deep inhale through your nose as you reach your arms out by your sides, palms facing forward, eventually coming into a prayer position over your head.

As you exhale, draw your palms down your midline to rest in front of your heart for a beat.

Release your arms down by your sides and repeat the cycle for three minutes.

Let your arms rest by your sides and relax for one minute.

Close your practice.

Journal.

NOTES

With each inhale, lengthen your spine toward the sky and imagine yourself growing taller. As you draw your hands to your heart, continue to keep your spine tall and press the soles of your feet into the earth.

Track the sensations in your body as you practice. Notice how full your breath becomes and if that changes anything in your body. Be sure to take notes on what you observed during your practice around those changes.

This is a great practice to do when you want to uplift yourself, cultivate a stronger life force presence, and remind yourself that you've got this. I recommend starting off trying it for a week in the morning before breakfast.

Sadness

Like happiness, sadness comes and goes. We often put so much pressure on ourselves to "be happy" that it can feel like there just isn't time in the day to address sadness that needs to be felt. As with physical pain, anger, or any other unpleasant feeling that we have to face, the breath is a key component for helping us face and hold space for ourselves in the middle of the discomfort.

Our culture is very quick to breeze by sadness and cover it up with another distraction. Next time you feel sad, instead of stuffing it down or trying to take the edge off, simply notice how you're breathing. This simple act of paying attention to your body in the middle of the unhappiness can begin to shift your awareness and give you an opportunity to lean into that feeling with support and strength.

As you learn to be with your sadness, you will find it easier to inquire about that emotion and get clear on what it is trying to tell you. Once you are clear on what that is, you have a much better chance of addressing it head-on. Now I'm not suggesting this as a way to breeze through the difficult emotion of sadness; I am, however, giving you an opportunity to get to the bottom of what is there so that you can continue to learn about yourself, grow, and eventually express what needs to come out so that it doesn't create emotional and energetic buildup in the body. Being able to be present with sadness is the doorway to greater resilience and the ability to self-heal whatever is troubling you.

Sadness

THE PRACTICE

Find a comfortable seat.

Set your practice intention.

Breathe slowly through your nose for a minute to settle in.

Next, take a couple of minutes to scan your body from head to toe, making note of any areas of comfort or discomfort.

Continue breathing deeply and slowly through your nose for eight minutes, allowing your body to breathe in whatever way that it wants to.

Notice the emotions as they come and go, anchoring yourself in the breath when you remember.

When finished, rest for a minute.

Close your practice.

Journal.

Often my clients start crying early on in the breathwork session when they come in sad or are having a tough time. There is something very powerful about stepping into a sacred, judgment-free space where they know they will be supported and attended to.

Sometimes crying is necessary and helpful during sessions as a way to cleanse and reset the system. If you find yourself crying during this practice, do not worry. Allow the emotions to rise and fall without hanging on to any of them. Let your body process how it needs to.

If you find that you are crying so deeply and you get caught up in stored memories, please use your breath to bring yourself back to the present time and consider reaching out to a practitioner for support.

If your sadness is persistent and chronic, I suggest working with a guide, whether that be a body-focused therapist or mind-body practitioner, to support you as you explore and uncover your feelings of sorrow.

Self-Healing

Often we are operating at such a fast pace in life that we don't take time to feel what needs to be felt in our bodies. The faster we move, the less opportunity our nervous system has to downshift and the more likely it is that feelings will begin to build up. The lack of parasympathetic nervous system engagement (rest-and-digest mode) coupled with an accumulation of unprocessed emotions makes it challenging for our bodies to heal in ways that are safe and regenerative.

The places in the body that are emotionally and energetically backlogged are likely to become areas of chronic pain and tension if they are not addressed on a consistent basis. It's widely known that eating nourishing foods, staying hydrated, and getting in some kind of movement each day is essential for our wellness. What is slowly gaining traction as well is the concept of taking care of our emotional well-being. This means having some kind of practice that connects us to how we're navigating our emotions so that we acknowledge, feel, process, and express them if needed.

The Self-Healing Breath is a practice that invites you to notice where your breath is moving freely in your body, where it feels stuck, where there might be energetic or emotional buildup, and where that buildup might manifest as a chronic holding pattern or area of pain. With your awareness and attention, the Self-Healing Breath can be a powerful tool to help deepen your body consciousness, release emotional blockages, and relieve pain to create more spaciousness and vitality in the body and breath.

Self-Healing

THE PRACTICE

Find a comfortable position.

Set your practice intention.

Breathe slowly through your nose for a minute to settle in.

Next, take a couple of minutes to scan your body from head to toe, making note of any areas of comfort or discomfort.

Choose one area of discomfort to support.

If accessible, bring one hand to that area and continue to breathe through the nose.

Allow yourself to notice any discomfort on the inhale as you soften your body on the exhale for several rounds.

Next, begin to lengthen your exhale by one to two counts.

Repeat this for six minutes on the same place on your body.

Notice any changes.

If you feel called to move to a different area of your body for the next five minutes, do so; otherwise, stay in the same place.

When finished, release your hand and rest for one to two minutes.

Sit up slowly.

Close your practice.

Journal.

If any emotions or sensations arise during this breathwork, allow them to be fully expressed as you move through the practice. If you get overwhelmed at any point, take a break. Open your eyes, look around the room, and when you're ready come back to the practice.

Once you are familiar with the Self-Healing Breath, here are some helpful inquiries to add to the body scan in the beginning: notice where the breath is moving freely in the body. Where does it feel stuck, blocked, dull, lifeless? When you come across an area of discomfort, explore the quality of the holding pattern.

The Self-Healing Breath is a powerful teacher in that it reminds us that nobody can do our work for us, that ultimately our bodies know how to heal themselves when given the attention, support, and nourishment they need. This practice is also very powerful because it teaches us to spend time with ourselves, to get to know where we're blocked and what our holding patterns are, and it gives us a tool to become more self-reliant in regard to our health and well-being.

Our current health care model is one that is often disempowering, and taking time to be with ourselves and our breath each day is a radical act of self-empowerment. In the words of one of my oldest teachers, we are our best healers.

Sleep

Like breath, sleep is one of life's necessities. But sleep is all too hard to come by for many people in this busy and full modern world. Quality sleep is linked to improved memory and brain function, emotional well-being, physical performance, stress reduction, quality of life, and personal safety. While you can find loads of articles online that share conflicting information on the number of hours of sleep humans need each night, and different suggestions for getting enough shut-eye, everyone agrees that it's the quality of sleep that takes precedence over the amount of hours in bed.

I've struggled off and on with insomnia in my adult life and have tried everything, including herbs, meditation, pharmaceuticals, blackout curtains, sex, earplugs, no electronics after 9 p.m., and some lesser-known practices like Reiki and delta wave music. After years of trying everything under the sun, I set out to develop a breath practice that would help me settle into sleep quickly and sleep until morning.

The Sleep Breath is a practice that slows down your heart rate while increasing oxygen in the bloodstream. It taps into your parasympathetic nervous system, responsible for your body's rest-and-digest mode, and works wonders to quiet the mind so that you can fall asleep with ease.

There are only a few practices where I suggest a breath hold, and this is one of them. The pause at the bottom of the exhale is important in the Sleep Breath as it is helps your parasympathetic nervous system slow down. Because our bodies are designed to breathe automatically, we will find a natural inhale at the end of our hold. So we don't even need to worry about the inhale; we can trust that it will come. The more you practice the Sleep Breath, the quicker it will bring you into a state of rest. The Sleep Breath is a staple practice for when you can't fall asleep or if you find yourself often waking up in the middle of the night. The state of our health is dependent on how well we sleep. This breath supports you to rest deeply so that you wake up refreshed and ready to begin the day.

Sleep

THE PRACTICE

Get in bed and make yourself comfortable.

Set your intention.

Begin breathing in and out through your nose slowly for a few rounds.

At the bottom of your exhale, pause for three to four counts.

Inhale, repeating the practice until you fall asleep.

Journal about your sleep in the morning.

Practice the Sleep Breath in bed, preferably with the lights off. Make your bedroom as cozy as possible so that you have a comfortable sleeping container. Setting an intention to sleep is very important. You want to let your body and mind know that you are committed to sleeping.

If holding your breath at the bottom of the exhale is new for you, go slow and don't force it. If you experience chronic stress or anxiety, chances are you don't breathe enough during the day and your breath might be shallow. The hold at the bottom of the exhale is an invitation take the breath deeper and slow it down. This might be uncomfortable in the beginning, and that is okay. Hold for just a count or two and work your way up. With practice you will be able to hold at the bottom of your exhale for longer, and the Sleep Breath will come with greater ease.

Unwind

As you're learning, changing your breathing pattern is a very effective and quick way to change your state. In the case of stress, which we all experience, learning how to unwind is an underrated and essential tool for changing our state to one of health and restoration.

We are under more stress than ever before in history. Just to boggle your mind for a moment, 90 percent of the world's data was created in the last two years. With the increasing amount of information available to us via email and smartphones, it's no wonder so many people struggle to stay grounded and relaxed.

In the section entitled "Breath: The Foundational Tool," I talked about how few people actually know how to relieve their stress and often mix up relaxing with checking out, numbing, or stuffing down what's happening. The Unwind Breath is the antidote to stress and is a healthy way to relax, discharge energy, and bring our bodies into a state of alignment.

The Unwind Breath is a nod to the ancient yogic practice of alternate nostril breathing, one of the first pranayama techniques I learned in my early twenties. In this practice, you alternate taking full breaths with each nostril with the help of your hands. The Unwind Breath is a powerful practice that de-escalates stress, provides quick calm, and lowers blood pressure. It also helps to balance energy centers in the body, which is key for relieving pressure in the mind and body.

It's easy to get overwhelmed and feel overloaded these days, and it's vital that we have a handy practice in our pocket to support our nervous systems to uncoil themselves in times of stress. I remember hearing from a teacher years ago that stress isn't bad or negative; it's our relationship to stress that matters. The Unwind Breath is a call to take charge of our health by giving our minds and bodies a safe space to release and reorganize.

Unwind

THE PRACTICE

Sit in a comfortable position with a tall spine and relaxed hips.

Set your practice intention.

Release any tension from your jaw.

Rest your left hand on your left knee, palm facing upward.

Gently place your right ring finger on the left nostril and your right thumb on the right nostril. Fold your second and middle fingers down to the palm of your hand and relax your little finger.

Take a deep breath through your nose and exhale out of your mouth. Close your right nostril with your thumb and slowly inhale through your left nostril. Close the left nostril with your thumb and hold your breath for a beat.

Release your right nostril and exhale slowly. Pause. Repeat on the alternate side to complete one cycle of the Unwind Breath.

Practice for five to ten rounds, alternating the breath between nostrils.

Release the practice and return your hands to your lap.

Breathe and rest for a minute, noticing any changes.

Close your practice.

Journal.

NOTES

Remember to always inhale through the opposite nostril you just exhaled through. Five rounds are a standard place to begin; you can go up to ten as you get more familiar with the practice.

Consistency with the breath is helpful with the Unwind Breath. Try to match the length of your inhales, pauses, and exhales for a smoother practice. An easy way to begin is to inhale for three counts, hold for three, exhale for three, and hold again for three. As you get comfortable and familiar with the practice you can increase your count and pay closer attention to the subtleties of the effects.

Do not force your breath in this practice, or any of the practices in this book. It's important to keep the breath moving in and out through the nose. Keep your fingers light on the face while practicing; pressure is not necessary.

The Unwind Breath can be tricky at first, so be patient with yourself. It gets easier with practice and time. The Unwind Breath is also ideal to practice before meditation.

ACKNOWLEDGMENTS

I am deeply grateful to those who made this lifelong dream come true and for those who supported me through this incredible, humbling journey. To my editor at Ten Speed Press, Kelly Snowden, who saw a space in the world for this book and helped refine the words to weave in the accessibility and depth that comes from these practices. To the incredible team that made *How To Breathe* come to life: Kara Plikaitis for her willingness to work with my distinct visual ideas; Emma Campion for taking a chance on this project; Jessica Comingore, who inspired the look and feel of this book; Erin Scott, whose dedication and unwavering encouragement for me to write this book made it possible; and Anaïs and Dax, who captured the tone and feeling of the imagery.

To my agent, Laura Lee Mattingly, who saw my vision, helped me refine it, and made this process seamless and fun. I am so grateful you believed in my work and my ability to write this book from the beginning.

Thank you to my parents, who recognized my creativity from an early age and fully supported my choices to carve out my own path. Thank you, Mom, for teaching me how to listen, set boundaries, and ask for more. Thank you, Dad, for reminding me that if I put my head down and work hard all that I dream of is possible. Thank you, brother, for showing me that life is so fragile and short and it's how we live each moment that matters.

To my heart, Nic, for loving me and supporting all my visions, no matter how out there. Thank you for being willing to show up for the messy and sometimes painful experiences we share—navigating what it means to be in conscious partnership. Thank you for taking care of yourself and thank you for stepping into this wild parenthood journey with me. To the golden child in my belly whom we cannot wait to meet, support, and love.

To the women who are my pillars, who are always keeping it real: Erica Chidi Cohen for showing me unconditional love and acceptance and for always getting me, even in moments when I don't fully get myself; Kelly LeVeque for showing me what generosity feels like and for always cheering me on; Trinity Troft for listening without judgment and reminding me how far I've come; Lacy Phillips for encouraging me to take risks and reminding me I have the answers within; Megan Attore for showing up for all the things and being part of my family; Suzanne Hall for believing that my voice matters and encouraging me to follow my heart.

To my community of teachers and healers who supported every aspect of my internal processes and shaped the teacher I am today: Tony Giuliano, Amy Mitchell, Aileen LaPierre, Thea Nathan, Jason Handler, and Dave Berger. To my dedicated and inspiring clients, students, and journal readers who show up and do the work of going within.

Thank you to the lineage of women writers who came before me and didn't have the kinds of opportunities that I have been given to share my work. Thank you to my community of extended family and friends who have continued to show up and support my work in the world.

Ten Speed Press and the Ten Speed Press colophon are registered trademarks of
Penguin Random House LLC.

Library of Congress Cataloging-in-Publication Data
Names: Neese, Ashley, 1980- author.
Title: How to breathe : 25 simple practices for calm, joy, and
    resilience / by Ashley Neese ; photography by Anaïs & Dax.
Description: California : Ten Speed Press, [2018] | Includes index. |
Identifiers: LCCN 2018038936 (print) | LCCN 2018039738 (ebook)
Subjects: LCSH: Breathing exercises—Health aspects. | BISAC: SELF-HELP /
    Meditations. | SELF-HELP / Spiritual. | SELF-HELP / Personal Growth /
    General.
Classification: LCC RA782 (ebook) | LCC RA782 .N42 2018 (print) |
    DDC 613/.192—dc23
LC record available at https://lccn.loc.gov/2018038936

Hardcover ISBN: 978-0-399-58271-4
eBook ISBN: 978-0-399-58272-1

Printed in China

Design by Kara Plikaitis

10 9 8 7 6 5 4 3 2 1

First Edition